Meet Yeshua

FIND THE HUMAN JESUS HIDING BEHIND THE CHRISTOLOGY

John I. Shonle

2011

Many Paths Publishing

Amherst, NH

Meet Yeshua: Find the Human Jesus Hiding behind the Christology

"One Mountain, Many Paths"

EAN 9780615369402
ISBN 978-0-615-36940-2
LCCN 2011910205
Many Paths Publishing, Amherst, NH

Table of Contents

Introduction

WHY ANOTHER BOOK ON JESUS?

This book was written primarily for Unitarian Universalists by someone who has been a Unitarian[1] at heart for over sixty years. However, others may find this book of interest. I am thinking especially of Muslims, for whom Jesus was a prophet but not divine. Likewise, Jewish people who might want a presentation of Jesus without a Christian overlay may find it appealing. Only the most liberal of the trinitarian Christians, perhaps inspired by the writings of Bishop John Shelby Spong and similar writers and looking for a modern interpretation of Jesus, will appreciate what I have to say. More traditional Christians, especially biblical literalists, will disagree strongly with much of what is written here. If any of them should happen to read this book, I hope that they will be open to, or at least tolerate, a different view of Jesus.

From time to time, I will refer to a concept as "Unitarian" rather than using the current designation "Unitarian Universalist." I am not trying to slight our Universalist traditions; rather, I am harking back to the origins of the two movements, which joined much later. The Unitarian movement started with rejection of the trinity, so when I call something "Unitarian," I want to emphasize the rejection of the trinitarian belief. Universalists originally were trinitarian, but they believed that everyone would be redeemed. In any case, they were devoted to acting on the teachings of Jesus, which is what I emphasize in this book.

....
1   I was a Unitarian well before the merger.

Jesus Christ! If you are like me, you had a knee-jerk reaction or a tightening of your gut with those words. Many Unitarian Universalists (UUs), according to my observation, dislike any mention of Jesus Christ and reject considering Jesus, even without "Christ" being added. Because of all my former negative associations with "Christ" and along with it the name "Jesus," and for historical accuracy, I will switch to using the Aramaic version of his name, "Yeshua," in the later parts of this book. While the emphasis in this book is on his human side, in the third, closing part, I try to make some sense of the christological myths.[2]

From what I have observed, most Unitarian Universalists know very little about Jesus the human teacher. If they were raised in a trinitarian church, they mostly heard about "Christ" and not so much about Jesus the teacher. If UUs were raised outside of a trinitarian setting, they often heard almost nothing. Jesus is largely ignored in many Unitarian Universalist churches, perhaps because of our rejection of his divinity. Somehow, Jesus seems to have disappeared along with "Christ." I know that there was a time when I did not want to hear anything about Jesus, with or without the added title.[3] Since Unitarian Universalists state in our principles that our sources include "Words and deeds of prophetic women and men... [and] Jewish and Christian teachings," we should not throw the baby out with the bathwater by overlooking such an important teacher.

Many things led me to write this book. I wondered why Christianity spread so fast and widely. Was I missing something? I then began to ponder what I might gain by examining the teachings of Jesus and their meaning for me today. I initially found it difficult to separate the teacher from the mythical character found in Christianity. My first thought was that there would be nothing left at all after I stripped away the christology.

My interest in the non-trinitarian Jesus grew during a trip to visit our partner church in Transylvania, where Unitarianism got its real start. Every Unitarian church there boldly states: *Egy Az Isten*—God Is One. However, Jesus is not ignored there—he just is not deified. Similarly, I needed only to look at my own church (in Milford, NH, built starting in

----

2 I use "myth" and its related forms in the sense of a founding story that has value, whether literally true or not.

3 "Christ" is strictly a title, coming from the Greek translation of the Hebrew "messiah," meaning an "anointed one." Chapter 9 discusses the meaning of "Christ" more thoroughly.

1870) to see that Jesus was very important in its early history, appearing in our stained glass windows, for example.

Many Christian churches focus almost entirely on a theologized "Christ" and often ignore Jesus' message. To be a little unkind, I think that some of the Christian churches are "the Church of Paul about a mythical Christ figure." Several observers agree with the idea that the Christian churches of today have more to do with Paul than with Jesus, a point that I elaborate in chapter 2.

The late Harvard professor and Christian minister Peter Gomes made a similar observation: "[Jesus] came preaching not himself but something to which he himself pointed, and in our zeal to crown him as the content of our preaching, most of us have failed to give due deference to the content of his preaching." And also, "We do not preach what Jesus preached. Instead, we preach Jesus" [Gomes pp 17 and 42]. It is a case of confusing the finger pointing to the moon with the moon itself, to use a Buddhist saying. However, in my experience, many Unitarian Universalist churches ignore both the *messenger* and the *message*. Where did the teachings of Jesus go? This book is my attempt to examine these teachings from a Unitarian Universalist viewpoint.

I did not remain in a creedal faith, but I am familiar with the Apostles' Creed. Let me quote a section of it, where the reference is to Jesus.

Who was conceived of the Holy Spirit,
born of the Virgin Mary,
suffered under Pontius Pilate,
was crucified, died, and was buried.

The Nicene Creed has similar wording in its corresponding section. Now, did you ever wonder what happened between "born" and "died"? The only details about the life of Jesus in the creeds are his birth and crucifixion. What about the rest of his life? What about all of his teachings? Are they worth nothing? I think not.

I am the sort who is curious about things. What was it about this man and his teachings that inspired such faith? You never would know from the creeds! A series on PBS, *From Jesus to Christ*, increased my curiosity. I became determined to find out if there was a human Jesus lurking behind all of the christology.

I also needed to separate my understanding of Jesus from some of the later actions of the Christian church done in his name: the brutality of the Crusades and the Inquisitions, the persecution of Jews based on incorrect stories in the bible, the justification of slavery, the reduction of women to the property of their husbands, and so on. Some of this intolerance continues today. One example is the denial by some churches of a woman's right to control her reproductive processes. Some pulpits preach the hatred of homosexuality. The so-called religious right has used the name of Jesus (or Christ) to justify its various stands. But when I heard Jesus invoked as justification for war, inequality, and discrimination, I felt that this was not consistent with what little I then knew of him. Books by Obery Hendricks, Robin Meyers (2006), Dan Wakefield, and Jim Wallis develop this point. So here was another reason to try to get back to the actual words and deeds of this teacher: I needed to separate what Jesus really said and stood for from all of the fundamentalist rhetoric.

Speaking for myself (although I imagine that many Unitarian Universalists share this trait), I was quite willing to accept the teachings of many people: the Buddha, Lao-Tzu, Thich Nhat Hanh, and so on. But I stubbornly did not want to hear about the teachings of Jesus. While I thought that I had an open mind, here was a case of a deeply seated bias. I had my head in the sand on this issue: don't preach Christ to me! Prior to my research for this book, I was not able to separate the teachings of the human Jesus from statements about Christ.

I felt that I needed some sort of resolution regarding Jesus. I could not understand where the resurrection, birth, and miracle stories came from. But mostly I wanted to know who this person known as Jesus really was. I wondered if Jesus could fit into my Unitarian Universalist thinking. Of course I cannot speak for all Unitarian Universalists, and my conclusions are not official positions of the Unitarian Universalist Association. This book is a report on my studies in search of some sort of resolution about Jesus that would fit my own Unitarian understanding.

Other writers have raised questions similar to mine about the life and teachings of Jesus. The introduction and first chapter of Erik Wikstrom's book, *Teacher, Guide, Companion: rediscovering Jesus in a secular world,* cover many of the same issues that I have raised here. The series of books by Bishop John Shelby Spong (see the Bibliography for two of them), who questions our understanding of Jesus in contemporary times, also crosses similar ground. My interpretation of Jesus differs somewhat from theirs. Other books that direct readers away from

"Christ" and back to Jesus include Philip Gulley, *If the Church Were Christian*, and Robin Meyers (2009), *Saving Jesus from the Church*.

Keep in mind while reading this book that I am expressing primarily my considered interpretation. I do not claim that my view is the only one. There is no such thing as a single "correct interpretation." It is fine if you disagree with me. I sincerely hope that my discussion will stimulate you to form your own picture of this man whom I call Yeshua.

FILTERS

I am not a biblical scholar versed in biblical Greek, Hebrew, Aramaic, and Coptic. Thus, I have had to rely on the works of others. Choosing which authors to read reflects a bias. As some have said, when you go looking for the historical Jesus, you find the Jesus you are seeking. I started this project with no preconceived image, really not knowing what I would find. I was uncertain that there would be anything at all after the christology was discarded. However, as my research continued, my image of Jesus became clearer—and my biases became stronger.

In looking at any data, a researcher uses filters, sometimes explicitly stated but other times perhaps not even recognized by the researcher. Here are some filters that I am aware of having and the effect each has brought. The first filter is a product of my training as a scientist. I expect things that occur in this universe to be explainable by the laws of nature. I believe there is a fundamental regularity in the way the universe runs that is not subject to being overruled by a god. Thus, I look for rational explanations rather than invoking divine intervention. I reject miracles. I acknowledge that there are things for which we do not currently have explanations, but I do not therefore need to invoke the intervention of a god. I certainly do not believe that things happen because of the "will of god."

Next, I do not belong to a creedal faith system that puts belief above rationality. I am not a trinitarian, but a Unitarian, so I reject christological concepts such as "Son of God," divine virgin birth, resurrection, "Savior," and a second coming. I do not believe in an apocalyptic final judgment day with an end to life as we know it. Heaven and hell are here on earth in the minds of people. So I filter out all apocalyptic statements. I do look at some of the "filtered" concepts as allegories or metaphors that have a non-literal value. But I freely admit that this book reflects my findings upon looking at Jesus through a Unitarian Universalist lens.

HOW THIS BOOK IS ORGANIZED

There are three principal parts to this book. Part I, *Getting Started*, has background information that puts the rest of the book into perspective. Readers eager to get right to my main message about Jesus as seen from a Unitarian Universalist vantage point can skip this first part without much loss of intelligibility.

Chapter 1, "The Time and Place," establishes the setting in which Jesus lived. It looks at the historical and religious background from early times up to the first century CE. Readers who get glassy-eyed when confronted with history could omit this chapter during a first reading, although later chapters of this book occasionally refer to this material. Chapter 2, "Source Material," discusses how we can know anything at all about Jesus the person. The process of stripping away the christology starts in this chapter.

Part II is mostly self-contained, so it could be a starting point for some readers. Entitled *Meet Yeshua*, it contains the heart of my message, which is about Jesus the completely human teacher. This is where I switch to using his Aramaic name, Yeshua, though I continue to refer to the christological figure as Jesus and retain that name in quotations. The chapters in Part II cover what is known about Yeshua, his sayings, and my interpretation of him using my Unitarian Universalist outlook. I do feel that these four chapters should be read in order. Readers who have jumped to Part II may wish to refer to chapter 1 for the historical setting and chapter 2 for my sources of information about this man. For a deeper understanding of who Yeshua was and what he did, I point readers to the discussion in chapter 8 on miracles, since there is some truth to the healings.

Part III, called *But What About…?*, looks at some of the christological questions that readers may still have. These chapters examine the myths surrounding Jesus' birth, miracles, and death. Readers whose curiosity centers on these myths and who want to see them from a Unitarian Universalist perspective could jump directly to this part. I feel that chapter 8 holds especially meaningful insights beyond the stories of the miracles.

The Appendix contains a guide for using this book in an Adult Religious Education class.

ABOUT ME

Any book is as much about the author as it is about the subject. In telling you more about myself, I will reveal more reasons for this book. I was raised a Presbyterian, faithfully attending Sunday school and then church most weeks. Somewhere around age eleven or twelve, I started doubting and then outright rejecting the whole trinity concept, including Jesus Christ. I could not accept the birth story, the miracles, and the resurrection as things that could have happened. I rejected the entire "Christ" concept, and Jesus along with it. I later became uncomfortable with the mere mention of "Jesus" in a church, even without "Christ" added, since it brought up "baggage."

When I was thirteen, I visited the All Souls Unitarian Church in Indianapolis. Its creed was the most marvelous thing I had ever heard (up until that time) in a church: "Love is the spirit of this church and service is its law—to dwell together in peace, to seek the truth in love, and to help one another; this is our covenant." I was especially taken by the phrase "...to seek the truth in love..." I felt I was given permission to be a seeker and not just an unquestioning believer. It was finally all right to ask questions! After this defining experience, I attended Unitarian or Unitarian Universalist churches in five states off and on for the next sixty-plus years—with occasional side trips, including a stint as a non-atarian.

I earned a PhD in physics and had a career in science—hence I seek rational explanations, not miracles. However, I have come to realize that there is much to life beyond what science can quantify. There are other modes of understanding. Science and religion are not in conflict, since (properly) they ask different questions. The trouble arises when one tries to answer the questions of the other.

It is important to realize that science can never answer the question why, but only the question how. Science describes how things are: for example, how objects move under the influence of gravity. But why do they do so? One might be tempted to answer that it is because of Newton's Law of Gravity. But why is that? Well, Einstein's theory of General Relativity says that matter causes a distortion of space-time. But why is that? Every time a more complete theory, such as string theory, supplies an answer to the question of why, we can still, much like a five-year-old, ask why without end. But all along science is describing ever more accurately *how* things move.

Scientists must have a basic faith, whether they recognize it or not. We take it as a fundamental that there is an underlying regularity to the universe: the laws of nature do not change chaotically. However, there is absolutely no way that we can ever prove this belief! We cannot do an experiment to prove the future. However, our understanding of this regularity becomes more accurate over time, as noted above.

I was struck by a passage from Matthew during a reading at a liberal UCC church I attended for a few years. In the Scholars' Version[4] of the gospels, we have:

> You may remember, I was hungry and you gave me something to eat; I was thirsty and you gave me something to drink; I was a foreigner and you showed me hospitality; I was naked and you clothed me; I was ill and you visited me; I was in prison and you came to see me...I swear to you, whatever you did for the most inconspicuous members of my family, you did for me as well. [Matt 25:35–36, 40b]

This basic message of caring for others remains with me as a guiding principle, of which I often fall short.

I spent several years studying Buddhism and adopted the parts that seem right for me. I still use some Buddhist ideas in my life. I know that there are still other valid expressions of religion. As many people have said, there is one mountain with many paths. I like to extend this image by picturing the top of the mountain as shrouded in clouds. We can only speculate about what is at the end of all our paths. Unfortunately, some people seem to think they have absolute knowledge of what is there. Even worse are those who stand at the bottom of the mountain shouting that their path is the only one that reaches the top.

....

4 The term "Scholars' Version" refers to the new translation of the gospels by the Jesus Seminar (*The Complete Gospels*, edited by Robert Miller). See chapter 2 for more information on the Jesus Seminar. I find that this rendition of the gospels fits my understanding of Jesus better than other versions, so all quotes from the gospels are from the Scholars' Version unless specified otherwise. All other biblical quotes are from the New Revised Standard Version (NRSV) bible.

The word "God" is used many times in this book, in a variety of meanings and, of course, in quotations. I use the uppercase "God" to refer to the entity that Jesus believed in. Sometimes I use the lowercase "god" as shorthand for my complex striving for an understanding. I do not believe in a god who intervenes in this world, especially not to act with vengeance or to alter the laws of nature as a favor for someone. I long ago rejected a theistic[5] view of god. I cannot imagine god blessing America or any other country: it is inconceivable to me that god takes sides. I do believe there is some sort of an underlying spirit of love and goodness, which I sometimes call the "Universal Spirit." I sense that there is something beyond us, guiding in a non-intervening fashion.

I particularly connect the presence of this Universal Spirit to my sense of awe, such as when I am gazing at the sky on a dark, clear night. This awe is expanded when I look at pictures from deep space that show many hundreds of galaxies in just a tiny region of the sky. Altogether, there are about a hundred billion galaxies, each with an average of about a hundred billion stars. This fact is so awe-inspiring that I cannot get my mind entirely around it. Certainly, this vast universe was not created for the benefit of humanity, and especially not for me! And when I look up at the stars, I am reminded that we all are stardust. Originally, the universe consisted mainly of hydrogen; most of the elements needed for life were not there. They had to be created deep inside stars. Some of these elements become available for life only when a supernova explodes, creating still more of the needed heavier elements and then scattering them out into space. Some of that stardust found its way to what became earth and eventually us.

Another form of spirituality arises when I am quietly sitting by a mountain stream or a waterfall, or watching the ocean from the shore, just being. The feelings that arise from enjoying music and the visual arts are more examples. There is an indefinable peace in being alone at the top of a tall mountain (14,000 feet is really inspiring). Unconditional love, such as a child gives, is on this list.

This spirit is everywhere and nowhere. My ideas of what "god" is—or the "Universal Spirit," or whatever name you may choose for

----

5 I am using "theism" in the narrow sense of the "father in the sky" who can intervene in this world, changing nature and rewarding or punishing people. See the books by Bishop John Shelby Spong for a lengthy discussion of the end of theism.

the *unnamable*—continue to change. I am now leaning toward "god is a verb." And this conception will probably evolve into something else.

I view my spiritual life as a journey. The quest is what is important. Once you stop asking questions, you are a spiritual zombie. I am even so bold as to say I know the meaning of life: it is to ask the question "What is the meaning of life?" and then to keep asking this question over and over.

ACKNOWLEDGMENTS

I have read many books on the subject of Jesus. While I have attempted to give complete attribution to all authors, I am sure that I have unconsciously used the wording of some authors, so I will give a general acknowledgement here. Please see the Bibliography for the scholars whose work I have utilized, whether consciously with proper attribution or unwittingly, recalling something and thinking that it was my own invention.

I wish to thank my team at CreateSpace for their tremendous help with editing the manuscript, interior layout, and cover design.

PERMISSIONS

MAP OF PALESTINE IN THE FIRST CENTURY CE

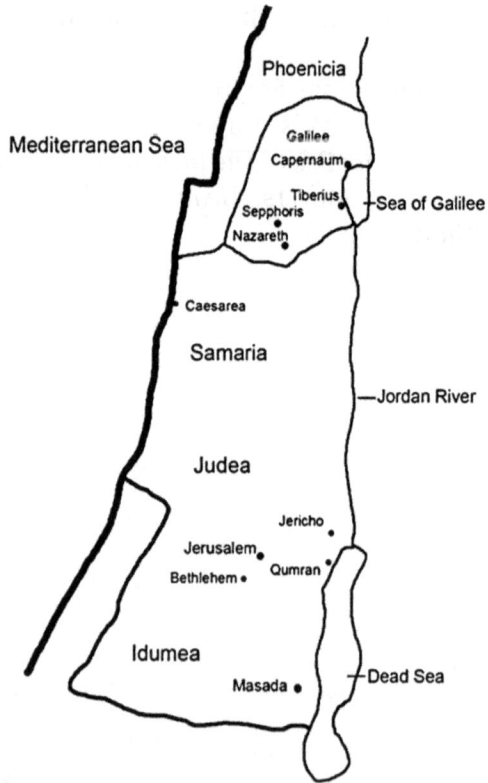

Phoenicia

Mediterranean Sea

Galilee

Capernaum

Tiberius

Sepphoris

Nazareth

Sea of Galilee

Caesarea

Samaria

Jordan River

Judea

Jericho

Jerusalem

Qumran

Bethlehem

Idumea

Masada

Dead Sea

This map is meant to be schematic only and not to a reliable scale.

Chapter 1:
The Time and Place

A BRIEF EARLY HISTORY OF THE JEWISH PEOPLE

It is not possible to comprehend Jesus fully if we use only our twenty-first-century perspective. For a proper understanding of him, we must consider the times and conditions during the life of Jesus. Jesus was a Jew (a fact that often seems to be overlooked) who lived in Palestine during the first part of the first century CE. I am indebted to Karen Armstrong [Armstrong 2007 chs 1–2] and Rodney Stark [Stark 2007 ch 4] for much of the following information. Another good reference is Armstrong's *A History of God* [Armstrong 1993 chs 1–2]. I also refer readers to the summary by Amy-Jill Levine [Levine et al. eds pp 14–24]. Virtually nothing about ancient Israel is without several possible interpretations. What I am presenting below is only one view, although mostly the majority one. I recommend the book *Ancient Israel*, edited by Hershel Shanks [Shanks ed 2011], for a wider presentation of the varying positions. There is far too much detail for the purposes of this book.

The starting point for understanding the conditions in Palestine in the first part of the first century is the early history of the Jewish people. At the root of Jewish traditions is a belief that a covenant with God establishes the Jewish people as his chosen people, and that the land of Israel was given to them after their escape from Egypt. Strictly, they held that the land was God's, but they were allowed to use it forever, believing that God would watch over them and protect them. So the Jewish people's identification with their land has a long, deep tradition.

The Hebrew Testament is written as if it were a historical record of the Israelites, a mode of writing that is highly unusual for a religious document. Many people believe that it represents an accurate record; however, it is difficult to separate actual history from legend. Even more to the point, the events were rewritten to emphasize theological points rather than historical ones. The books of the Hebrew Testament were written and rewritten in a very different order from the way they now appear in the bible, with some of the earliest "history" written well after some of the other books. While scholarship shows that many of the wars, kings, and so on in the Hebrew Testament are found in various other records, other parts of the Hebrew Testament find no such support.

Much of the early history reported in the first two books of the Hebrew Testament (Genesis and Exodus) is just story. Perhaps the most important story for the Jewish people is the exodus from Egypt. Scholars disagree as to how much of the exodus account is based on fact. It is so basic to the Jewish people that it probably does rest on some factual happenings, which have become mixed with legend. Archaeology has yet to find supporting evidence for the exodus story [Armstrong 2007 p 15]. The region that was then called Canaan was under Egyptian control from about the nineteenth to about the fourteenth century BCE. Becoming free from Egypt may indeed have seemed like a return from captivity. The evidence for Moses is mixed. Egyptian writings hold no record of him or the exodus. However, "Moses" is an Egyptian, not Semitic, name.

Some biblical details seem to confirm that there was such a person as Moses [Stark 2007 p 174]. However,, the "forty years of wandering" probably has no basis; "forty" was often used to represent a large number, as in "It rained forty days and forty nights." One source suggests that the escapees stayed camped in one spot for thirty-eight years. Very likely, some of the early people were nomads, which may explain the story of wandering. Another example is the archaeological evidence that shows that the Jewish peoples[1] settled peacefully in the Canaanite highlands—there was no "Joshua and the battle of Jericho." Archaeologists have shown that some walls of ancient Jericho did fall, but not because of a battle.

A more accurate history of Israel begins in about the eleventh or twelfth century BCE in Palestine, with the twelve tribes. There is some

----

1 There may have been a small number of slaves who came from Egypt, but many other people melded into what became the Israelites: Midianites, Moabites, Jebusites, Gibeonites, Hebrews, Kenites, and possibly others [Stark 2007 p 172].

doubt about when all twelve tribes came into existence. Initially the Israelites set up a representational governing council of judges instead of kings. Obery Hendricks Jr. emphasizes that not having a king but recognizing only the rule of God was radical for that era [Hendricks p 18].

Around 1020 BCE the Israelites asked Samuel to appoint a king in place of his sons, who were corrupt judges. Samuel was reluctant to do this and warned the people that they would regret this change when some later king became a tyrant. [1 Sam 8] Saul was the first king. It is significant that Samuel anointed Saul's head with oil [1 Sam 10:1], since the strict meaning of "messiah" is "one who has been anointed." There were no divine overtones to the word. Some priests and prophets were also anointed. In addition, according to tradition, on the day of his anointment, a king became an adopted "son of god" [Ps 2:7].

The tribes of Israel were united under the successive kings Saul, David, and Solomon during the period from about 1020 to 920 BCE. The historical record becomes somewhat better as we go from Saul to David to Solomon. In much later times, David became the model of what a messiah (anointed king) should be: a liberator who delivers the people of Israel from oppressors [Hendricks p 24].

Solomon built the first Temple in Jerusalem. Strict monotheism was not practiced at that time: his many wives had a variety of religions, and he erected shrines for each religion. After the death of Solomon, Israel split into two kingdoms: Israel in the north with ten tribes, and Judea in the south with two tribes (Judah and Benjamin). This split led to the development of two somewhat different biblical stories and two different names for god: "Elohim" (northern) and "YHVH" (southern).

Most of the northern kingdom was conquered by Assyria in 722 BCE, and many people were deported. Once they became assimilated into their new surroundings, they became known as the ten lost tribes. Some people from the northern kingdom were able to flee to Judea, bringing their biblical traditions with them. The two versions were combined, leading to two different and sometimes contradictory versions of the same story in the Hebrew Testament. For example, there are two versions of the story of Adam and Eve [Gen 1:26–31 and 2:7–23].

Polytheism was widely practiced from the eleventh to the sixth centuries BCE. Even Solomon's Temple had idols to other gods. The God of the Jewish people was the most important one, not necessarily the only one. The first commandment says, "You shall have no other gods before me," [Exod. 20:3] indicating only that YHVH was to be in first place. Karen Armstrong states that the bible shows that polytheism lasted until after the destruction of the Temple in 586 BCE [Armstrong 2007 p 16]. References to plural gods appear in many parts of the Hebrew Testament. Psalm 82 has God take his place in a council with other gods. Psalm 135:5b says, "Our Lord is above all gods." Genesis 1:26 uses the plural "let us make mankind..." The earliest mention of the name YHVH may be that in Judges 5, dating perhaps from the eleventh century BCE [Stark 2007 p 175]. Meanwhile Baal, the god of agriculture, was very popular. It is not at all clear whether the Ten Commandments were even generally known at that time.

A strict monotheism may have started as early as the time of Samuel but was not generally practiced. Monotheism grew only slowly. In the eighth century BCE, there were prophets who called for a rejection of all other gods. This was a time of peace and prosperity, but a large gap had arisen between the rich and poor. These prophets were also calling for a change from this inequality. The books of Amos (mostly concerned with injustice), Hosea, and Jeremiah cover this period. This era is thus an important precedent for the situation in Jesus' time and indeed has validity for today.

In the late seventh century BCE, an old scroll was found during a renovation of the Temple. This scroll, attributed to Moses, contained the foundation for the Law. Before that time, there had been no Sabbath, no Passover nor any of the dietary laws [Stark 2007 p 184]. This scroll became the basis for the books called Deuteronomy and Leviticus.

The southern kingdom (Judea) was conquered by the Babylonians under Nebuchadnezzar in 597 BCE, and many of the ruling and upper-class Judeans were taken off to Babylonia in captivity. The Temple in Jerusalem was destroyed a little later, in 586 BCE. The destruction of the Temple was symbolically significant, since it was the center of both religion and the state. It was basic to the Jewish practice of that time, since God was said to dwell in the Temple. Atonements had to be made by sacrifice there. When things did not go according to God's plan, such as the terrible events that led to defeat, the prophets said that it was because of the sinfulness of the people, who had turned from God and his Law. The destruction of the first Temple was foretold by Jeremiah [7:12–15] because of corruption (although this could have been a case of writing done later to make this a "prediction after the fact").

The time of exile in Babylonia was very important for the development of the Hebrew Testament as we now know it. With the destruction of the Temple, the earlier traditions had to be modified to allow for worship elsewhere. The old scriptures were edited and new material added, perhaps from oral traditions. The history of the development of the bible is too lengthy to include here [see Karen Armstrong 2007]. Many scholars detect the influence of Zoroastrianism in some of these additions, especially with the start of ideas about life after death and resurrection. The major legends of the early years took form as the book of Genesis. Ezekiel and the two prophets known as second and third Isaiah are from the Babylonian period. The Jewish religion in some semblance of what we know today was born there. Rodney Stark calls the people who returned from the Babylonian exile "genuine Jews" [Stark 2007 p 186].

Subsequently, the Persians conquered the Babylonians in 538 BCE. It was their policy to let captured people return to their homeland, so the Judeans were permitted to return (though still under Persian rule), although some stayed behind in Babylonia. Not all Judeans had been taken into captivity. Those who had stayed behind, mostly of the lower class, resented the returning exiles since the returnees reclaimed much of the land that had formerly been theirs. They also clashed over religion, since so much had changed in Babylonia but not in Judea.

The Temple in Jerusalem was rebuilt within a few decades, possibly using some Persian money. During this time the Torah (the first five books of the Hebrew Testament, also called the Law) was again revised to take its present form, more or less. Even so, not until the time of Ezra, around 400 BCE, did the average person hear about the Law as it became enforced as the law of the land [Armstrong 2007 pp 32–35].

The holiness code in Leviticus stresses actions. Among many other things, the Law established rights for widows, orphans, and the poor. A portion of each crop was to be left for the poor. The Law included a provision for debt forgiveness every seven years during a yearlong "Sabbath." This debt forgiveness did not happen during times of foreign domination—especially under the Romans, since most of the debt was owed to the occupiers. Keeping the Sabbath day is part of the Ten Commandments. It is more than just a time for God. It is a temporary state of equality among the people. Everyone behaves in the same limited manner (at least ideally).

After the return from exile in Babylonia, the high priest became the intermediary between the people and God. At the same time, the high priest was also the liaison between the people and whoever was occupying the country. The priests were thus in a very powerful position and later took advantage of their position to become quite wealthy. Tithing was started then and developed into a large source of income for the priests.

Samaria (which had been part of the northern kingdom) was partly settled by non-Jewish people after the Assyrian conquest of 722 BCE. Some of these people adopted Judaism. The Babylonians had not taken Samarian people into exile. Sometime after the destruction of the Jerusalem Temple, the Samaritans built their own Temple on Mt. Gerizim. The Judeans who had returned from Babylonia considered the Samaritans to be apostates who were racially impure. The gospels hold many references to the resulting prejudice against the Samaritans. The Temple in Samaria was destroyed by the Hasmoneans (see below) in 135 BCE, a further reason for hostility between the two regions.

Alexander the Great (331–302 BCE) conquered much of the Mediterranean world and parts of the Middle East, including Palestine. Following this conquest, a cultural shift brought Greek ideas and language into the conquered territory. The gospels were originally written in Greek, and they reveal other Greek influences as well. The Greek translation of the Hebrew Testament, rather than the original Hebrew-language one, was a major source for the gospel writers. Greek mythology and philosophy influenced the ideas of some writers of that time, when many Jewish people moved or were displaced into various major cities of the Greek empire. These relocated Jews, adding to those who remained behind in Babylonia, became known as the diaspora.

After the death of Alexander, his empire became fragmented. The lands of Palestine were first conquered by the Hellenistic Ptolemys (302–198 BCE), followed by Hellenistic Seleucids (198–167 BCE). Intolerable conditions during the reign of Antiochus IV, especially concerning the defilement of the Temple and his attempt to force Greek traditions on the Jews, led to a successful revolt under the leadership of the Hasmonean family, begun in 167 BCE. They were not in complete control until 142 BCE. The Hasmoneans, also known as the Maccabees, enlarged the land under their control to about the size of David's kingdom. This included re-annexing Galilee, which had been part of the northern kingdom, around 100 BCE. Contrary to the Jewish tradition of a hereditary priesthood, the Hasmoneans installed themselves as the high priests. Because many Jews objected to this flouting of tradition, splinter sects of Judaism abounded during this time.

Independence did not last long: the Romans took over in 63 BCE during a time of internal conflict between two of the Hasmonean brothers. The Romans appointed several local governors and installed Herod as king of Judea in 37 BCE. Under Herod, Judea was a semi-autonomous state in the Roman Empire. Herod added significantly to the Temple and ordered many other constructions, but none in Galilee. He was hated by many because he was from Idumaea and was considered to be only half-Jewish, and also because of his cruelties and high taxes. When Herod died in 4 BCE, his kingdom was divided among his three sons.

Antipas received Galilee and ruled until 39 CE. His rule was mostly calm. Under the agreement with Rome, "tribute" (taxes, for all practical purposes) was paid to Rome, but no Roman troops were stationed in Galilee. Archelaus, who received Judea, Samaria, and Idumaea, did not rule well and was removed by the Romans. Significantly, these regions were then placed under direct Roman rule, with the high priests appointed by the Romans. Pontius Pilate, the most famous of the Roman prefects in Judea, ruled from 26 to 36 CE.

The Romans did not control all of the local details; this was the task of the high priest in Jerusalem and his council, the Sanhedrin, with the Temple guards acting as the police of Jerusalem. The priests were very rich and held much land in the time of Jesus. The point of contact between the populace and the Romans remained the high priests, whose connection to Rome made it easy for them to rid themselves of anyone rocking the boat [Hendricks p 59]. But people were also afraid to oppose the priesthood for fear of God's vengeance, since the priests were thought to be God's representatives on earth.

The mix of cultures in Judea in this period had an important influence on both the people and the religion. Jewish, Roman, and Greek cultures and traditions clashed, while Judaism, whether the Jews liked it or not, was heavily influenced by the foreign occupations, especially the Greek [Crossan 1991 p 418].

General unrest prevailed in Judea from perhaps 40 BCE to the revolt of 66–70 CE. (Some authorities, however, contend that the reports of unrest as given in the history written by Josephus are exaggerated.)

There was a major conflict following the death of Herod in 4 BCE, followed by another, minor revolt in 6 CE. At least two massive nonviolent demonstrations stopped Roman attempts to put pagan symbols inside the Temple. The Romans were impressed by the demonstrators' willingness to die passively rather than betray their faith. On a smaller but continuing scale, "bandits" (who were dispossessed people fighting back) launched frequent attacks on the Romans and their Jewish collaborators. The Jews, of course, wished for independence and a return to the former conditions as a theocracy. But they mostly expected God to step in and make things right.

A significant event for both the Jews and nascent Christianity was the destruction of the Temple in 70 CE near the end of a major, unsuccessful revolt against Roman rule. This was consequential for the development of both Rabbinical Judaism and Christianity, because in the absence of the Temple and its priests, the Pharisaic branch (see below) became more prominent, eventually evolving into the rabbinic system. This same event led the Jesus cults increasingly to split from Judaism. Karen Armstrong notes that Christianity would be very different if the Temple had not been destroyed by the Romans [Armstrong 2007 p 55]. The emerging Christians held the destruction of the Temple to be a repudiation of the former Jewish ways or even retaliation for the crucifixion of Jesus.

After the fall of Jerusalem, many Jews were deported, adding to the already existing diaspora. One last unsuccessful revolt against Rome between 132 and 135 CE led to the complete eviction of all Jews from Jerusalem. Israel ceased to exist for the next eighteen centuries.

An overwhelming fact is that the Jewish people have had an independent state for only brief periods (historically speaking) in their entire history.

JEWISH INFLUENCES ON THE GOSPELS

The Hebrew Testament and other Jewish writings contain many precedents for some of the events reported in the gospels. According to these writings, Enoch went straight to heaven; Elijah multiplied a food supply, raised a person from the dead, and also went straight to heaven. Elisha cured a leper, multiplied food, and raised the dead. The two miracle workers Elijah and Elisha, who probably lived around 880–840 BCE, were from the northern part of Palestine, as Jesus was later on.

Other miracle workers were noted in Jewish literature. Honi the Circle Drawer (around 65 BCE) was noted for controlling rain. Hanina ben Dosa lived around the time of Jesus. Among other things, he healed a child from a distance. Alan Avery-Peck [in Levine et al. eds ch 8] takes a longer look at these two miracle workers, whose contemporaries held their piety to be the reason behind their success in asking God to do things. Other teachers and miracle workers were active outside of Judea during these times. Two examples are Apollonius of Tyana and Eleazar the exorcist. Some of the others are discussed by Wendy Cotter [Levine et al. eds ch 9]. I will talk more about miracles in chapter 8 of this book.

The Law was both a religious and a political reality after about 400 BCE. Certain things were absolutely forbidden, such as the behaviors prohibited in the Ten Commandments. But many other requirements, some spelled out in great detail, governed such decisions as what to eat and not eat, or how to cook and clean utensils. E. P. Sanders observes that Jewish law brought all of life under God, so that every activity became a worship of God [Sanders pp 37–38]. These restrictions made it impossible for the Jews in the diaspora to assimilate into the foreign cities in which they found themselves, since their lifestyle was so different.

The more restrictive parts of the Law were for the priestly class and the Sadducees, who were in charge of the Temple, but the Pharisees also followed them. The Pharisees, mentioned many times in the gospels, were a nonpriestly subgroup of Judaism who were very strict in observing the Law, extending the ideas of priestly purity to everyday living. They held that all the Jewish people were in a sense priests and thus could directly approach God. They had no power to enforce any of their views on others and in general did not try. Their role as adversaries to Jesus, found in the gospels, was a later retrojection; they had little presence in Galilee in the time of Jesus.

The Essenes were also very strict, going well beyond the Law. The documentation of them contains some contradictions as to how they lived and how many they were. Apparently there were several groups, with some in towns living a non-celibate life. The strictest group, judging the Temple system to be corrupt, had withdrawn to a remote location near the Dead Sea to wait for two messiahs, one a warrior and the other priestly. This group was celibate. Scholars disagree over whether they were the ones who hid the Dead Sea Scrolls in the caves at Qumran. There is no evidence that Jesus had any contact with them.

In the normal course of life, one would necessarily have to violate the Law, for example through contact with blood while slaughtering an animal, or contact with the dead during a burial. These and many other actions, such as engaging in sex, rendered a person temporarily unclean. There were prescribed ways to become clean again. On the other hand, some people, often referred to in the gospels as "lepers," were considered permanently unclean. This term does not refer what we call leprosy today but to a variety of ailments. Illnesses and disabilities were thought to result from either sins or demonic possession.

In addition, there were "sinners": people who deliberately broke some aspect of the Law without repenting and making sacrifice at the Temple to the God of the Jews, who was always ready to forgive the truly repentant.

The poorest people, who had to scratch just to stay alive, probably had little or no time for all of the niceties of the Law. The rich had time for such things as not working one full day a week and could easily fast twice a week since they did no manual labor. The priests were often quite caught up with the enforcement of the Law rather than caring for the common person.

In general, in contrast to the impression from the gospels, the Temple system was well run and not dishonest (but perhaps very greedy and self-centered). One of the main points of conflict concerning the Temple was that the priests were in a sense collaborators with the Romans.

The Hebrew Testament frequently characterizes calamities as punishments for the collective sins of the Jewish people, especially the worshiping of idols. "Satan" is referred to as an "adversary" in the earlier books (see the book of Job, for example), not a devil as in current usage. The idea of a devil came later, after the Babylonian captivity and the resulting Persian influence.

Around the time of Jesus, many Jews believed that God would soon keep his covenant with them, freeing them from foreign rule and establishing a Godly kingdom with the Temple at its center. While some expected God to do this for them, others looked for a messiah (anointed king) in the image of David who would lead them to victory over their enemies. This messiah was to be a military leader, a king to establish the final kingdom centered in Jerusalem. It was widely hoped this would happen soon, and numerous prophets foretold such a coming or even claimed to be that messiah. Many people performed healings and preached that the end of the corrupt world, to be replaced by life under the rule of God, was close at hand. A collection of writings known as the Psalms of Solomon, dating from the first century BCE, is particularly messianic.

The Pharisees believed in an afterlife, which was not a common notion in Judaism at that time. The Sadducees did not believe in resurrections. The Hebrew Testament contains very few references to a general life after death. The book of Zechariah talks about the righteous dead being restored to life at the end times [Wilson p 56]. Similar ideas are also found in Enoch 1, which may have been written by the Essenes about the time of Jesus.

GALILEE

Galilee was its own region, briefly united with Judea only twice during the ancient history of Palestine. It was not strictly Jewish, having been overrun by many cultures after about 700 BCE, each leaving some non-Jewish people and traditions behind. After the Assyrian conquest (722 BCE), Galilee had only a small population until about the second century BCE.

Galilee became part of Israel again around 100 BCE, after the Maccabees conquered the land. However, it was still geographically separated from Judea by Samaria. Galilee then became more Jewish with the (perhaps forced) conversions of some of the gentiles. Galilee was also resettled with a significant number of Jewish people from the diaspora. The Maccabees persuaded Jews from Babylonia and Persia to come to Galilee. These people who came back were called the "natzorim." Wayne-Daniel Berard speculates that this word maybe the origin of the town name "Nazareth" [Berard pp 26–27].

In the time of Jesus, Galilee still had a significant non-Jewish population, since only about a hundred years had passed since its reassimilation into Jewish control. Thus it was not only geographically separated but also somewhat culturally separated from Judea, where the Temple was. Galilee also had its own dialect of Aramaic. There had likely been intermarriage, so Judeans thought some Galileans were "racially impure" and looked down on them, though they disdained the Samaritans more. Because of the Galileans' relative isolation and freedom from direct Roman occupation, they were less influenced by the Greco-Roman culture than the residents of Judea and the gospel writers were. Despite the problems of being indirectly under Roman rule, Galilee enjoyed relative peace and freedom under Antipas from 4 BCE to 39 CE.

Sepphoris, a small city about four miles from Nazareth, was made the capital of the Galilean district in about 56 BCE. The extent to which Sepphoris was influenced by Greek and Roman cultures is the subject of robust debate. Some scholars hold that the Greco-Roman influence was substantial. Thus, Jesus might have learned Greek, seen plays, and in general might have had considerable knowledge of Greek traditions. The other view notes that most of the Greek and Roman structures and artifacts in Sepphoris date from after the life of Jesus, as Mark Chancey and Eric M. Meyers reported in the *Biblical Archaeology Review* [reprinted in Shanks ed 2006 pp 2–19]. A sidebar by Joseph A. Fitzmyer [ibid. p 16] holds that Greek was not a common language in that time and place. The bible does not refer to Sepphoris. The city was damaged during the uprising in 4 BCE but rebuilt almost immediately; recent archaeological findings indicate that the historian Josephus may have exaggerated the amount of damage. It is sheer speculation that Jesus might have worked there and been exposed to city life.

Tiberias was a new city, built around 20 CE on the shore of the Sea of Galilee to serve as the new capital. There was more of a mix of gentiles in Tiberias than in Sepphoris. The populations of these two cities in the first century CE, estimated at about 20,000 each, would have consumed most of the agricultural output of lower Galilee. A major east-west road ran from the Mediterranean Sea to Tiberias, but the village of Nazareth lay off the beaten track. Nazareth possibly had only 200-400 people in the first century CE.

Synagogues in Galilee in the early first century CE were most likely just meetings at a convenient location. The archeological evidence is ambiguous. Some researchers claim that four synagogues from the late-Temple days have been found in Galilee. However, others say that none of the remains found in Galilee are identifiable as dedicated synagogues during the time of Jesus [Jonathan Reed, in Levine et al. eds p 51].

GREEK AND ROMAN INFLUENCE

The theme of the dead returning and interacting with humans was common in the Greek and Roman religions. Gods and goddesses (according to legend) often assumed human form and interacted with humans for better or worse, sometimes mating with them. The resulting offspring were often the heroes of mythology. The gods and goddesses had human-like emotions and could act out in anger and retribution often with unpredictable whims, as exemplified in Homer's *Iliad*.

Greek philosophy held that there was some sort of an ultimate perfection, but because it was too perfect to interact with the base world, people invoked an intermediary, called Logos, as a go-between. The idea of Logos is echoed in the Hebrew Testament as Wisdom (who was female) and later in the gospel of John.

Antisthenes (born about 436 BCE and a pupil of Socrates) founded a philosophical movement that came to be known as Cynicism. ("Cynic" here should not be conflated with our current meaning of "cynical.") Diogenes of Sinope, who lived from about 400 to 320 BCE, was one of his followers. The Cynics held that there were no objects of knowledge but only what the individual sensed. Virtue was the ultimate truth, and pleasure was bad. Their basic idea was to denounce convention, especially materialism and authoritarian figures. One had to be free from desire, anger, and fear (which is reminiscent of certain Buddhist principles). By not having much of anything, the Cynics were free. They had only a small pouch to hold a few things, carried a staff, and wore a cloak off of one shoulder, but no shoes. But while the Cynics denounced society, they totally depended on it for survival by begging. They were itinerants and beggars, usually found in cities. They would as a rule travel about by themselves, spreading their message, mostly by example: "Live freely by living simply, as I do." (We should maybe pay some attention right now to this concept. There is a similar contemporary slogan: "Live simply that others may simply live.")

Science as we know it was almost nonexistent outside of the work of the Greek philosophers. Astrology was commonly believed. The cause of illness was not understood; sins or evil spirits were held to blame. The understanding of physics was wrong. Chemistry was not understood, although in about 400 BCE Democritus hypothesized that everything was composed of atoms.

Little is known about exactly how the average person viewed the world then, but we can surmise, from what was written and from views surviving into the Middle Ages, that the common worldview was that the earth consisted of a flat surface extending only a very limited distance beyond what a person knew. Underneath was a menacing "underworld," often identified as the place of the dead though not usually seen as a "hell" where the unrighteous were tormented. Above was a fixed dome, the "firmament," where the sun, moon, and stars traveled. Beyond was "heaven." This dome was thought to be only a short distance above the earth. Because of the closeness of the firmament, it made sense to think that stars could fall from the sky or that a star could hover above a town closely enough to identify it. However, some of the Greeks knew better (see End Note).

Aristotle held that justice was inherently unequal, and thus inequality was natural. The wealthy of the Greek and Roman empires seemed to endorse this concept (as do many of the wealthy today!). There was almost no middle class in the Roman Empire. It is estimated that perhaps 95 percent of the population ranked in the lowest economic stratum. Life was harsh for most people.

After the Roman political system became an empire, the emperor came to be viewed as the son of god who was raised to heaven at death. Julius Caesar had been deified at the time of his death in 40

BCE, and the title "son of god" was formally assumed by his adopted son Augustus and subsequent emperors. A miraculous birth story was added. The Roman occupation was therefore more than just a political and military event: there were religious overtones as well. The whole idea of the emperor as the son of god with a miraculous birth, ruling by divine right and rising to heaven, was possibly a source for some of the ideas of the emerging Christians. However, they needed to create a better story.

From time to time the Romans did persecute the Jews, but despite the strong religion of the empire, the Romans generally did not require the Jews to give up their religion or worship the Roman emperor because they recognized and honored the long traditions of the Jews.

However, the Roman concept of land as a commodity to be bought and sold contrasted strongly with the Jewish view that the land belonged to God and could not be sold. Under Roman control, the vast majority of farmland was consolidated in the hands of the wealthy. This led to the displacement of peasants from their ancestral lands. Traditionally, a farmer had raised only what was needed for his family, plus a little extra to sell for other necessities. This gradually changed as the needs of the cities grew and the peasants increasingly sold their crops to the towns. As time went on, this became less a case of "selling" and more a case of confiscation as payment of "taxes." Under this new system the peasants often ended deeply in debt and lost their land. Though not powerful enough to openly revolt, the peasant class was able to resist passively, for example by responding slowly to requests, not doing what was asked, hiding crops, and even engaging in minor sabotage.

A patronage system was the order of the day. Patrons could grant favors to their clients, and the clients in turn served and supported their patron. It was a pyramid of power: patrons were usually the client of someone above them, and their clients might be patrons to those below. The patronage system applied to both the sociopolitical and the religious spheres. Favor seekers had to go through well-defined channels. They could not directly approach someone near the top. The patron served as a broker, needing in turn to address his own patron until, if the supplicant were lucky, his concern reached the appropriate level.

. . . .

End Note

It can come as a surprise to learn that not only did the Greek astronomers know that the earth was a sphere, but in the third century BCE Eratosthenes determined its diameter rather accurately. Around the same time, Aristarchus estimated the distance to the moon as being something over 200,000 miles (close to the correct figure). He was not able to determine the distance to the sun but knew that it was great and thus the sun was much bigger than the earth. This knowledge led Aristarchus to be the first (that we know of) to put the sun at the center of the universe—a view that was not widely accepted at the time, of course. (The idea was revived by Copernicus [1473–1543] and Galileo [1564–1642].)

Chapter 2:
Source Material

INTRODUCTION

So, you want to learn about Jesus. Doesn't the bible provide a full account of his life in the books of Matthew and Luke? In a word, NO! Many religious people turn to the bible as their only source of information, whether they read it themselves or hear parts of it in church. A major problem is that usually only selected parts of the bible are read, leading to a distorted picture of even the few facts that are there. But the reason goes much deeper.

I take it as fundamental that the bible was written by humans for humans. It is not the "Divine Word of God" handed down from above. Authors write about their own understanding and beliefs, informed by many sources but not dictated by God. Marcus Borg emphasizes that the bible was not meant to be literal, but rather to be understood metaphorically. He considers metaphors to have an additional meaning that is more than literal and more than factual [Borg 2006 p 51].

Burton Mack often uses the term "mythmaking," but in the sense of the story of a people rather than as a pejorative dismissal of value. He says that the early Christian myths were appropriate and plausible for that time and place. It bears repeating that the bible must be viewed in the context of its times.

The Christian Testament did not spring into existence in one piece but came together only gradually from many possible choices. The four traditional gospels were selected from among many alternatives around 200 CE, mostly due to the work of Ireaeus. The decisions on which books to include in the full Testament were largely made in the mid-fourth century CE. The bible remained fluid into the fourteenth and fifteenth centuries. It was not until the printing press came into common use that the bible became more settled. It is worth noting that different branches of Christianity even today include different books in their bibles, and of course many different translations are used. No writings from the time of Jesus' life or immediately after have been found. When things were written down later, it was in the context of the messages that the authors were trying to convey to their immediate audiences, and not as history. Historical settings were either lost or ignored. We should keep in mind that because of the general illiteracy of the times, the bible was not meant to be read by the people but to be delivered orally.

I cannot emphasize too often that the writers of the bible had agendas. They were not historians but were rather trying to get theological points across. Thus, we cannot automatically assume that *anything* in the bible represents what actually happened; it must be carefully examined with this warning in mind.

PAUL

The earliest-written surviving accounts about Jesus are the letters of Paul, but even there we do not have the originals but only copies of copies, which were possibly altered in the process of copying, whether intentionally or accidentally. The letters were written roughly between 50 and 60 CE, before any of the gospels but about twenty to thirty years after the death of Jesus. Some of the letters that once were ascribed to Paul are now thought to have been written by his followers, using his name. Fully understanding Paul's letters poses a challenge because we have only one side of the correspondence. We can only infer what problems or questions the various communities might have had or asked. We should also keep in mind that Paul probably had a larger body to his theology and preaching than what is preserved in the few letters.

Paul did not know Jesus and did not have much contact with those who did. In fact, he proudly claims to have his knowledge directly! "For I want you to know, brothers and sisters, that the gospel that was proclaimed by me is not of human origin; for I did not receive it from a human source, nor was I taught it, but I received it through a revelation of Jesus Christ" [Gal 1:11–12]. Also, "We speak of these things in words not taught by human wisdom but taught by the Spirit" [1 Cor 2:13]. Such declarations certainly do not meet current standards as a reliable, verifiable, way of obtaining information, but we must assume that they seemed plausible at the time. In any event, such statements do not allow us to trace Paul's sources.

The stories about Paul in the book known as the Acts of the Apostles indicate that he knew some things about the early movements of Jesus, before his "conversion." We must suppose that he had some better source than "revelation," since there is agreement with some of the other later writings. However, some of this agreement was likely from the later writers adopting selected ideas of Paul. It is not clear whether the gospel writers saw the letters of Paul, heard about his teachings, or independently used a common source. For Paul, the death-and-resurrection story was all that mattered. "For I decided to know nothing among you except Jesus Christ, and him crucified" [1 Cor 2:2]. Paul mentioned nothing about the life of Jesus (except that he was born) and almost nothing of his teachings. However, several of Paul's statements are in accord with Jesus' ideas about equality and justice. Paul made little mention of an earthly kingdom of God, a concept that was central to Jesus, as we shall see in chapter 5. Paul instead often wrote about a resurrected afterlife in heaven.

The problem of Paul goes much deeper. Current Christianity is firmly grounded in the writings of Paul. Some scholars view much of Paul's theology to be his own creation. Karen Armstrong states that Christianity as we know it was the creation of Paul [Armstrong 1993 p 86]. Geza Vermes agrees, calling Paul a creative writer who, by altering or omitting the real message of Jesus, created the basis for Christianity [Vermes 2000 p 76]. Mostly Paul invented his theology based on his understanding of the meaning of Jesus' death. Barrie Wilson, in his book *How Jesus Became Christian*, gives one of the strongest cases for Paul having created a new religion that became Christianity. James Tabor, in *The Jesus Dynasty* [ch 16], argues along the same lines, though in a milder manner. Rex Weyler states that Paul may have been influenced by the Persian cult of Mithras, since many of the traditions that Paul introduced are similar to those of Mithraism, including the eucharist [Weyler pp 59–60]. So aside from not knowing Jesus, Paul also distorted the image of Jesus that I will be presenting later.

There were two main early pre-Christian groups based on Jesus, as well as several other, less influential ones (Rex Weyler lists about a dozen groups [Weyler p 50]). The "Jesus sect," based in Jerusalem and headed by Jesus' brother James, was tied to the Jewish tradition, including following the Torah. The life and sayings of Jesus were of major importance to them. John Dominic Crossan calls this the "life tradition." The other, the "Christ sect," appears to have been developed by Paul, perhaps based on imagined revelations and Hellenistic mystery cults. The writings of Paul created an image of the "dead-and-risen Christ" that is mostly contrary to the message of Jesus. This group, which Crossan calls the "death tradition," won the survival competition.

Paul made a clear break from the Torah. This move proved to be of major importance for recruiting gentiles, who largely did not want to follow all of the details of the Law.

The account about Paul given in the Christian Testament book called the Acts of the Apostles (written by the author known as Luke) is often at odds with Paul's own account. Barrie Wilson considers much of Acts to be a fiction of Luke [Wilson, especially ch 10], stating that the account in Acts was an attempt to give credence to Paul's new church by attempting to link the Christ movement to the Jesus movement.

Paul seemed to accept the suffering of the poor as something they had to bear, since everything was going to change soon. It was God who would make the change, not actions of the people. Thus Paul, so contrary to the example of Jesus, did not advocate doing anything to make things better. "Paul transformed Jesus' concern for the collective social, economic, and political deliverance for his entire people into an obsession with the personal piety of individuals" [Hendricks p 85]. However, Marcus Borg and John Dominic Crossan present a different and kinder picture of Paul that contradicts some of the above interpretations. In their opinion, Paul was very interested in equality [Borg and Crossan 2009].

So we learn next to nothing about Jesus the person from the earliest writings in the Christian Testament. Much of what Paul wrote leads us farther from Jesus and toward the mythical Christ figure. The pseudo–letters of Paul not only corrupt the message of Jesus even more but also skew the message of Paul.

THE GOSPELS

Chronologically, the next writings in the bible are the four gospels: Mark, Matthew, Luke, and John. Most scholars agree that the first gospel written was that of Mark (circa 70 to 74 CE), followed by Matthew (circa 80–85 CE), with Luke perhaps five years later and finally John (circa

90–100 CE). It is generally held that the first two and possibly Luke were written before the letters of Paul had been gathered, copied, and distributed. While the direct wording of Paul's letters was not used, the authors of Mark, Matthew, and especially Luke appear to have been familiar with Paul, based on their use of some of Paul's theology. Luke had a reasonable knowledge of Paul by the time he wrote Acts, which was well after he wrote his gospel. The gospel writers probably lived and worked in regions where Paul had taken his religious mission, so they could easily have had knowledge of Paul's preaching, if not his letters.

The gospels offer insight more into the ways in which Jesus was then understood and the times in which they were written than into the historical Jesus. We must never lose sight of the fact that the authors of the Christian Testament were concerned with presenting stories for their immediate audiences. They were after theological persuasion rather than history. We also need to be aware that the gospels were most likely written after the destruction of the Temple in Jerusalem in 70 CE, and that this event influenced the tone of their writings.

The earliest gospel, Mark, was probably written about forty years after the death of Jesus. None of the gospel writers had direct knowledge of him. We do not know the true names of the authors. Indeed, some of the gospels may have been written by a committee. The names of these books were assigned, using guesswork, probably in the mid second century CE. I will continue to use the attributed names for easy identification.

Writing a generation or two after Jesus' death, the authors of the gospels appear to have assumed that their contemporary situations applied also in the time of Jesus. For example, the exchanges in Galilee between Jesus and the Pharisees are the work of the gospel writers, since the Pharisees had no significant presence in early first-century Galilee. These supposed exchanges probably reflected later conflicts between the emerging Jesus cults and the Jewish establishment, which had become more Pharisaic after the fall of the Temple. The writers appear to have assumed that Jesus was as educated as they were and equally well acquainted with the Hebrew Testament. This assumption led them to put scriptural quotes in his mouth, often taken from the Greek translation, which Jesus would not have known. It was common for the members of a movement to ascribe new ideas to its founder, following a Greek tradition. Some of this activity was a deliberate attempt to show that the Hebrew Testament "predicted" the coming and death of Jesus. John Dominic Crossan often uses the expression "not history remembered but prophecy historicized" when referring to "events" in the gospels that were based on "predictions" from the Hebrew Testament. With the collapse of the Jewish state after the destruction of the Temple, the writers of the gospels wanted to make it seem as if Jesus was the proper continuation of the prophesies of the Hebrew Testament, leading to the redemption of not only the Jews but also the gentiles.

According to E. P. Sanders, the gospels are based on the idea that Jesus fulfilled some prophecies from the Hebrew Testament. Since it appeared to the writers to be true in some cases, they felt that it must be true for others, so they added new stories about Jesus that were based on the Hebrew Testament. They were not trying to be historically accurate but rather to create a new message [Sanders pp 84–85].

The first three gospels are called the synoptic[1] gospels, since they agree in many places. It is now thought that Mark was the first and that Matthew and Luke both had copies of Mark from which to work, but that they wrote independently of one another. Matthew and Luke also shared another source, which is now lost; it can only be inferred from the two texts (see "The Gospels of 'Q' and Thomas" below).

In understanding the gospels, especially the first three, we need to keep in mind that the authors, who thought that the "Kingdom of God" would be coming soon, were writing for the near future. Thus, we should not assume that anything written was meant to be a message for the indefinite future.

Geza Vermes, noting that biographic and narrative styles of transmitting theology are absent from the Hebrew Testament and the writings of the Essenes, concludes that the gospels are primarily based on Greek literary styles [Vermes 2003 p 19, especially footnote 28].

A thorough reading of the synoptic gospels shows that contemporary Christian churches are far from the spirit of these gospels. Jesus would probably be completely surprised at what has been and is now being said in his name, especially in the rest of the Christian Testament. Wayne-Daniel Berard states that the gospels are much closer to modern Judaism than to modern Christianity [Berard p 6]. He further notes that

----

1 From the Greek, "to look alike."

no other religion centers so much on the founder, rather than on the message of the founder [Berard p 212].

MARK

The author we know as Mark seems to have been non-Jewish, since he made some blunders about both Judaism and the geography of Palestine. Mark apparently did not have a good copy of the Hebrew Testament and thus garbled some of the quotations in it that appeared as words of Jesus. It seems that he was writing for a non-Jewish audience, since he often felt the need to explain Jewish words and traditions. He confused practices of his time (about 70 CE) with those of 30 CE. John Dominic Crossan suggests that maybe "Mark" was a woman [Crossan 1991 p 416]. Randel Helms thinks that Mark was at a second remove from Peter and third from Jesus [Helms p 4]. Thus we can safely say that this "Mark" was not the John Mark from Jerusalem who is mentioned in the bible.

Mark did not mean for his gospel to be a historical biography. He offered no birth story. His account of Jesus begins when the adult Jesus is starting his ministry. The sequence of actions and stories in Mark was almost certainly put together randomly from various bits in the oral tradition.[2] There is no assurance that Jesus' baptism even occurred before he started his ministry.

Mark focused more on miracles and exorcisms than on the sayings and parables that prevail in the other synoptics. Mark gave a more human face to Jesus than the other writers; for example, he often depicted Jesus as not knowing everything. The later gospels "corrected" that view. Geza Vermes notes that the gospel of Mark is probably closer to the historical Jesus than any other writing in the bible [Vermes 2000 p 235].

Mark portrayed the disciples as being thickheaded, since Jesus often had to repeat things and explain the parables. Of course, such a portrayal could have been an excuse to repeat the message. According to Mark, Jesus asked people not to reveal that he was the "Son of God." This list of people included his disciples, those whom he cured, and

---

2 The same observation—about the lack of a reliable chronology for the events in Jesus' life, aside from being sandwiched between an imagined beginning and his death—applies to the other gospels as well. There is nothing in the bible that approaches a biography.

even demons. Since the purpose of a gospel is to deliver "good news" (the literal meaning of "gospel"), one would think that the "Son of God" message would have been an open declaration. Mark's quest for secrecy is very reminiscent of the Greek "mystery cults." Since Mark seems to have been non-Jewish, it is reasonable to suppose that he was indeed familiar with these.

Burton Mack thinks the entire story of Jesus' last days and death is an invention of Mark [Mack 1995 pp 156–158]. Many other scholars agree. For example, Wayne-Daniel Berard says that Mark's gospel was created as propaganda to influence his audience [Berard p 155]. The destruction of the Temple in 70 CE was a dividing point for Judaism. Mark, writing after the destruction of the Temple, wanted to reinterpret the Jewish traditions with Jesus as the final prophet, so his death had to be portrayed as special. I will discuss Jesus' death more completely in chapter 9.

Most scholars think that the gospel of Mark originally ended at 16:8, with no post-death appearances of Jesus, and that verses 16:9–20 were added later to include several such appearances in keeping with the later gospels. Later additions are definite in John and probable in Matthew and Luke as well.

MATTHEW

Matthew was probably the most Jewish of the gospel writers. His group likely was a Jewish sect at odds with the Pharisees [White p 24]. He was writing later than Mark and thus stood even more removed from the original oral traditions. Matthew clearly had a copy of Mark's gospel, as he used about 90 percent of it. He did "correct" Mark in places by using more accurate quotes from the Hebrew Testament and an "improved" theology for Jesus. In addition, he used at least one or two other sources.

One of Matthew's main aims was to link Jesus to Moses and to "prophecies" in the Hebrew Testament. "The Jesus story was actually composed with the Hebrew scriptures open, and the memory of Jesus was actually adapted to conform to biblical expectations" [Spong 2007 p 144]. Matthew created events in the life of Jesus to match writings in the Hebrew bible so that things happened "according to the scriptures." His idea was that the Hebrew Testament was specifically all about predictions of the life of Jesus, and thus Jesus was the epitome of all

Jewish history. Of course, Matthew had to do some fancy scrambling to make things fit. Further, by viewing scripture primarily as a collection of prophecies awaiting fulfillment, Matthew could implicitly expose the "incompleteness" of Judaism.

Some passages show that Matthew's movement not only was familiar with the teachings of Paul but considered them incorrect, since Paul had set the Torah aside [Wilson p 151]. It is very likely that the following passage refers specifically to Paul.

> [Jesus speaking] Don't imagine that I have come to annul the Law or the Prophets. I have come not to annul but to fulfill. I swear to you, before the world disappears, not one iota, not one serif, will disappear from the Law, until that happens. *Whoever ignores one of the most trivial of these regulations, and teaches others to do so,* will be called trivial in Heaven's domain. [Matt 5:17–19, emphasis added]

We cannot leave the gospel of Matthew without noting that a birth story was added. Some scholars believe that the gospel of Matthew originally began at chapter 3—in the same time frame where Mark's account began, with the story of John the Baptizer—and that the birth story in the first two chapters may have been added later. The Greek and Roman mythologies all required that a leader or godlike figure have a remarkable birth. Apparently, Matthew or a later author kindly obliged. The birth story will be discussed more in chapter 7.

LUKE

Luke also copied from the gospel of Mark and changed it, but he used only about half of Mark. Luke also wrote a companion work called "The Acts of the Apostles" ("Acts" for short). It is generally thought that Luke had not seen Matthew's work. However, there is the problem that both Matthew and Luke, in telling their own nativity stories, used the same birthplace (Bethlehem), the idea of a Davidic lineage, and the names of Jesus' parents (Joseph and Mary), suggesting that Luke may have copied Matthew. (The accounts of the birth are otherwise quite distinct; these discrepancies will be taken up in chapter 7.) If Matthew's birth narrative was added later by someone who had seen Luke's gospel, the foregoing problem disappears. Alternatively, rather than Luke copying from Matthew, there may have been an independent myth of the birth that both writers knew.

The similarities of many of the sayings given in Matthew and Luke, apart from the evident copying from Mark, have led to the suggestion that they shared another common written source, the "Q gospel," which is discussed in a later section of this chapter. Both Matthew and Luke may also have had other independent sources.

It has been suggested that Luke saw at least some of the writings of Paul. The writer of both of Luke's books, especially Acts, was clearly acquainted with the theology and life of Paul, since about half of Acts concerns Paul. Luke's account of Paul is often at odds with what is in Paul's letters.

Many authorities think that Luke was a gentile but very well acquainted with the Hebrew Testament. The wording of the quotations Luke used indicates that he knew only the Greek version, not the one written in Hebrew. Possibly Luke was a non-Jewish "God Fearer" at a synagogue in the diaspora. These were open to non-Jews who were interested in the Jewish God but did not want to convert [White p 247]. Helms [p 80] speculates that Luke may even have been raised in an early Christian community and that "Luke" was a woman, possibly even a gentile Christian widow [Helms pp 61–66]. Luke, like Mark, often made mistakes about the geography of Palestine.

JOHN

The gospel of John will get little attention in this book. Its author introduced a very different theology for Jesus. There is no consensus on how much John was influenced by the earlier gospels, since he deviated so much from them [see Meier vol 1 p 44, for example]. The book of John was written in a very different style, likely reflecting the influence of Greek philosophy, probably for an intellectual Greek-speaking audience. The author apparently had at least some knowledge of Luke and Mark. He ignored the birth stories of Matthew and Luke and said instead that Jesus was "Logos," in existence since the beginning of time.

However, some scholars think that John also had an independent source that may have been more correct as to certain historical items. For example, in the account of John, the Last Supper and subsequent events take place a day earlier than in the other gospels, which avoids the problem of conflict with the observance of Passover that the other gospels have. I will come back to this point in chapter 9. More pertinent for the life of Jesus, John indicated that Jesus went to Jerusalem at least three times, whereas Mark and Matthew had him make only the one final trip. Luke mentioned the final trip and one other trip when Jesus was twelve.

Randel Helms believes that "John" was written in three layers by different people [Helms p 114]. L. Michael White, on the other hand, detects five layers to John [White p 307]. I refer you to the works cited for more details on the layers.

Most scholars agree that at least chapter 21 of John was a later addition. It is written in a different style, introduces future eschatology, and adds baptism and the eucharist [Helms p 154]. The "throw the first stone" story (John 7:53–8:11) is almost certainly an insertion by later copiers. Found in different places in various early copies, this passage interrupts the flow of the text on either side of it in the position where it is now found in the book of John. Verses 1–5, 9–14, and 16–18 of John's chapter 1 are also thought to be additions.

John thought that "signs" (miracles) were important and thus listed seven miracles, some of them similar to ones in the synoptics. Note the use of the sacred number seven. Randel Helms thinks that John may have had another source for the miracles, now lost, which Helms names the "signs gospel" [Helms pp 114–115]. An attempted reconstruction of the "signs gospel" appears in *The Complete Gospels* [Miller ed. pp 180–193].

John's gospel features few of the sayings found in the synoptics but introduces many new "sayings," such as the "I am..." series, which includes "I am the light of the world...I am the bread of life...I am the authentic vine." A number of scholars, such as the Jesus Seminar, Robert Price, and Geza Vermes, contend that none of these sayings is authentic.

In spite of, or perhaps because of, all of the major differences between John and the synoptics, the gospel of John is a major source for many Christian churches, since it focuses so heavily on the christology. It is only a slight exaggeration to say that John, along with Paul, *created* most current Christian beliefs—for example, "I am the way, and I am truth, and I am life...No one gets to the Father unless it is through me" [John 14:6]. Then there is the oft-quoted verse John 3:16b, "God gave up an only son, so that every one who believes in him will not be lost but have real life." By focusing on believing in the Christ figure as the only way to salvation, churches can more easily skip over what I think is the real message of Jesus: to be sharing, helping, and caring. As a simplification, the synoptic gospels are about Jesus and John is about Christ. See chapters 4 and 5 for a fuller discussion of Jesus' message.

OTHER PROBLEMS WITH THE BIBLICAL SOURCES

The gospels are not reliable sources.[3] The earliest surviving manuscripts are copies of copies. Scholars date the earliest known copies of the gospels to the third century CE. Many changes were made in the process of hand copying over the centuries before the printing press. The late Robert Funk estimated that there are more than 70,000 significant variations in the old Greek manuscripts of the Christian Testament [Funk 1996 p 94].

Some of these changes were unintentional, but others were deliberate and reflect the needs of the church as it evolved. This subject is discussed at length in Bart Ehrman's *Misquoting Jesus: The Story Behind Who Changed the Bible and Why*. See also Randel Helms, *Who Wrote the Gospels*, and Burton Mack, *Who Wrote the New Testament*. Scholars have identified additions to the gospels made by later editors.

Another reason not to take the bible as history is its many inconsistencies, sometimes even within a single book. People who take the bible as "the word of God" tend to ignore the problem of God not being consistent. I point to only a few examples of this here, as a complete discussion would fill another book. Inconsistencies in the birth stories, already mentioned, are further discussed in chapter 7. What were the disciples' names? The End Note in chapter 3 presents more information on this point. The accounts of Paul's mission in Acts differ markedly from those in Paul's letters. What were the final words of Jesus? The bible gives at least three distinct renditions—four, counting one that appears in some versions of Luke (see my chapter 9 for details).

Then we have the variances among the different English translations, which in some cases lead to different images. The well-loved "King James" version is a bad translation of a very late, much-altered

---

3 Of course, some people will refute this statement with an argument along these lines: "God said it. I believe it. End of story."

text. Some people apparently believe that Jesus even spoke King James English—perhaps out of a wish to ascribe to him the beauty of its language, which *is* poetic. Then there are the New English, the Standard, New Standard, and the New Revised Standard editions of the bible, to name a few. Different bibles include different books as their canon.

The present-day bible contains only four gospels, but originally there were many writings. Once Paul's church spread to include gentiles, and the Jesus cults began increasingly to separate from Judaism, the early church evolved in many directions. Multiple gospels were written for the various emerging sects, reflecting the needs and understanding of the places and times. Fierce disagreements arose over these writings. As some sects grew stronger, they railed against the others, calling them heretics. Some of these alternative gospels survive only in fragments or even merely as texts mentioned by other writers. Today many scholars believe that we must consider all of the early gospels, not just the "approved" canonical ones. Bart Ehrman's *Lost Scriptures: Books that Did Not Make It into the New Testament* discusses some of these books. Translations of some of these "lost" gospels appear in *The Complete Gospels* [Robert Miller, ed].

OTHER FACTORS

The earliest churches were "Jesus movements" within Judaism. Only later, especially after the destruction of the Temple, did these Jesus sects separate from Judaism. Paul's mission to Greek-speaking cities changed the evolution of Christianity, making some impact from Greek culture almost unavoidable. Burton Mack, referring mostly to Paul's church, notes that early Christianity was influenced by the religions of late antiquity, with features taken from Greek myths of dying and rising gods, baptism, and sacred meals [Mack 1993 p 22].

The bible was never intended to be "history," as some now think of it, but rather was meant as "story." In addition to not knowing the actual names of the authors of the gospels, we do not know where or for what audience they were written. Were they written by Jews for Jews? Mark and Luke may have been gentiles; John, writing for a Greek-speaking gentile audience, was even more likely to have been a non-Jew. Matthew was probably a Jew with a "Jesus cult" Jewish audience.

It is generally accepted that the Jesus movements in the cities of the diaspora initially centered on synagogues, with a Jewish and sometimes a gentile audience. The Christian Testament was originally written in Greek, with no known writings in either Hebrew or Aramaic, although the book called Matthew may originally have been written in Hebrew or even Aramaic, or possibly later translated into one of them. One idea, well expounded by John Shelby Spong [1996], is that the synoptic gospels were written as weekly lessons for the synagogues in the midrash[4] tradition, following the order of the Jewish liturgical year. They thus were never intended to be "history" but rather are stories relating the new Jesus movements to the familiar Hebrew Testament readings.

HISTORICAL SOURCES

There is no good historical documentation of Jesus. The well-educated historian Josephus, born a Jew in 37 CE, wrote several histories of the Jewish people after he had defected to the Romans, including two major, overlapping histories of the period 175 BCE to 66 CE. Variations between these two accounts (and a third minor one) cause scholars to question his accuracy.

His accounts mention Jesus only a few times.

> About this time there lived Jesus, a wise man. For he was one who wrought surprising feats and was a teacher of such people as accept the truth gladly. He won over many Jews and many of the Greeks. When Pilate, upon hearing him accused by men of the highest standing amongst us, had condemned him to be crucified, those who had in the first place come to love him did not give up their affection for him. And the tribe of Christians, so called after him, has still to this day not disappeared. [Crossan 1994 p161, quoting from Josephus' *Antiquities*, but with certain parts thought to have been interpolated by later Christian scribes removed by Crossan]

In another place, Josephus mentioned "a man named James, the brother of Jesus who was called Christ." Otherwise Josephus paid

---

4 The term "midrash" refers to explanatory material used to expand and clarify the biblical text that was used on a given day.

little attention to Jesus, devoting only 13 lines to him as contrasted to 27 lines for his brother James and 24 lines for John the Baptizer. Neither Paul nor Peter is named in his histories [Crossan and Reed p 32], although there is mention of a Saul who could be the biblical Paul [Weyler p 43].

Tacitus, in a history from the early second century CE, mentioned that "Christus" had been executed by Pilate.

Celsus, a Roman philosopher writing around 180 CE, mentioned Jesus but derided the notion that a person of lower class could possibly have been born of a virgin or be divine—that is, he did not question the birth or divinity but only doubted that they could occur in such a low-class person [Crossan 1994 p 27].

The Dead Sea Scrolls contribute only indirectly to understanding Jesus, by showing what some of the Jewish traditions were like during his life. Peter Flint, in his "Jesus and the Dead Sea Scrolls" [Levine et al. eds ch 6, especially pp 112 and 115], quotes a scroll from the first century BCE that talks about God fathering a messiah, and a blessing using bread and wine. There is little overlap between the scrolls and the teachings of Jesus, aside from some sayings that were common at that time. However, the Dead Sea Scrolls bear some similarity to what some of the gospel authors wrote many years after Jesus' death.

The scrolls also contain fragments of two extra-biblical books, Enoch I and II, which date from about 350 BCE to 50 CE and may or may not be associated with the Essenes. A translation of a translation also exists. These books hold many mentions of a coming "chosen one" who resembles the image of Jesus created by the later writers. George Nickelsburg says that some of the Enochian community became members of the early Christian movement and used these traditions in describing Jesus [Levine et al. eds p 91].

The historical literature concerning the Persian god Mithras parallels some parts of the gospels to such an extent that some writers have suggested that Mithraism had some influence on the gospels. Both stories feature the concept of being "born again," sacred meals using wine and bread with "body and blood" symbolism, and a dying and rising god, as Marvin Meyer points out in "The Mithras Liturgy" [Levine et al. eds ch 10].

THE DIDACHE

The Didache, meaning "the teachings," was an instruction manual for converts to the early church. A copy of it, dating from about 1050, was found in 1873 in a library. The original may have dated back to the first century CE. Earlier scholarship held that the Didache was dependent on the gospels, but more recent thought considers it largely independent of either the gospels or Paul—at least in its earliest layers. Like many other early writings, it appears that there are several layers in it, as people added and revised the document over the years.

Aaron Milavec thinks that the Didache dates from the mid first century and is thus older than, and independent from, the gospels [Milavec pp ix and xiii]. However, some striking similarities to Matthew appear in the third section of the Didache. Similarities to the gospels are also observable in sections 13 and 14. The last section (16) is quite apocalyptic. These sections were likely later insertions. In any case, the Didache does include a few of the sayings of Jesus, especially in the first section [Milavec pp 3–5]. These sayings appear to be in an early format.

The Didache gives better insight into how the early church functioned and how the early Christians lived than anything found in the Christian Testament [Milavec p ix]. I will come back to the Didache in chapter 9, since it provides some interesting descriptions of the eucharist that indicate an early origin for this book.

THE GOSPELS OF "Q" AND THOMAS

So where do we get any information about Jesus? One way is to look to what Jesus did and taught. We must use the gospels, even if they are flawed. In addition, certain "helper" texts enable scholars to sort out what might be authentic sayings of Jesus from the creations of the gospel writers.

One such source is the "Q Gospel," inferred from Matthew and Luke. Obviously, both Matthew and Luke saw and copied parts of Mark. At the same time, both Matthew and Luke included much material that was not found in Mark, mostly in the form of sayings and parables. Some of these passages have almost identical Greek wording in these two books. The crucial point is whether Luke ever saw the gospel that Matthew wrote. Most scholars think that he did not. Since their writings were in

Greek but the original sayings of Jesus would have been in Aramaic, these additions, given their striking similarities, could only have come from a common written Greek source to which both authors had access.

The first suggestion of some source common to Matthew and Luke was in 1838. The hypothesis became more prominent with the work of H. J. Holtzmann in 1863. Johannes Weiss coined the name "Q" in 1890, coming from the German word *Quelle*, which means source. More recently, scholars such as John Kloppenberg and Burton Mack have divided Q into three levels, separating the earliest traditions from the later additions. Because the Q sayings, especially "level one," are thought to be closely related to the actual teachings of Jesus, I have been influenced by this collection. For reconstructions of Q, see James Robinson, *The Gospel of Jesus*, and Burton Mack, *The Lost Gospel of Q*. It is a pity that there are no surviving texts.

Not everyone accepts the Q hypothesis, which requires believing that Luke saw and copied from the gospel of Matthew. Support for the Q hypothesis is found in the Didache sayings and in the gospel of Thomas (see below), which made the idea of a "sayings only" gospel more plausible. The Q gospel has no details of Jesus' birth, life, or death. The second and third levels do introduce miracles and an eschatological outlook.

Robert Price notes that some of the Q^1-level sayings resemble sayings of the Cynics [Price p 214]. Burton Mack thinks that the earliest Jesus sect was the Q group, who added sayings as time went on. As previously noted, adding new "sayings" follows a Greek tradition. The image of Jesus then went from that of a teacher to an apocalyptic prophet, and the story of John the Baptizer was added in the Q^2 level. The Q^3 level was probably added after the fall of Jerusalem.

Another source is the gospel of Thomas, which was not written in a narrative style but mostly as a collection of sayings. A manuscript, written in Coptic and dating from perhaps the third or fourth century CE, was found among many other manuscripts in Egypt in 1945. However, Thomas is thought to be a copy of a much earlier text, partly because of its agreement with some early fragments of text in Greek. Additional evidence for an early date for Thomas comes from the considerable overlap with the sayings of the Q text. This overlap also helps reinforce the idea of Q as a sayings gospel. Some of the Thomas gospel was probably added later by the gnostics. John Meier points out parallels between

Thomas and Matthew that indicate that at least some of Thomas was written later than Matthew. He also notes other passages that appear similar [Meier vol 1 pp 135–139]. However, this does not prove copying since there could easily have been a common source used by both. The gospel of Thomas has no birth stories or any of the death tradition.

Regarding the change between the early works and the later writings, Robert Funk observed that "[t]he two early sayings gospels, Q and Thomas, permit us to reconstruct, to a limited extent, what the religion *of* Jesus must have been—as distinguished from the religion *about* Jesus" [Funk 1996 p 41, emphasis in original].

Two other non-canonical gospels are sometimes used: The Secret Gospel of Mark (which exists only in a few verses written in another book, which might even be a later forgery) and a fragment of the Gospel of Peter. John Dominic Crossan notably made use of the latter in his discussion of the resurrection myth.

Much of current Christian theology was introduced well after the time of the writing of the bible. The concept of the Trinity is not found in the bible. The Catholic Church claims equal validity for the postbiblical writings.

USING THE SAYINGS

So how do we navigate through all of this information and misinformation? In trying to sort out the man, Jesus, from the myth, I started with the work of the Jesus Seminar about who he was, as defined by what he actually said and did. The Jesus Seminar, composed of about seventy-five biblical scholars along with many Associates, assembled as many of the earliest available sources as they could, retranslated the gospels, and produced two books: *The Five Gospels* and *The Acts of Jesus*. (The fifth gospel was that of Thomas.) The Jesus Seminarians voted on the likelihood that any saying or deed was authentically that of Jesus (though not in the sense that their selections were the actual words). Having started there, I went on to use many other sources and insights.

Not all scholars agree with the Jesus Seminar's view, and their reactions to this work represent a wide diversity of opinion. Craig Blomberg has stated that the Seminar's view of Jesus is not sufficiently Jewish to be valid [quoted in Berard p 4]. This is why I also looked to Geza Vermes.

Geza Vermes, who is Jewish,[5] has independently assessed the sayings of Jesus [Vermes 2004]. The remarkable thing is not that there are some differences, but that the Jesus Seminar and Vermes agree so much, since Vermes was not a member of the Jesus Seminar and used somewhat different criteria. I will come back to the selections of the Jesus Seminar and Geza Vermes in chapters 4 and 5.

At one extreme of the diversity of opinion, we have fundamentalists saying that every word in the gospels is literally and factually correct. At the other end, we have Robert Price, who makes the case that virtually none of the sayings attributed to Jesus originated with him, and that Luke composed all of the parables that appear only in his gospel. He also claims that the ones that are in only Matthew came from Jewish traditions and not Jesus [Price pp 173–174].

Jesus did not have to originate all of his sayings in order to have them noted. Some of the reported sayings can indeed be traced to earlier traditions. He must have been an effective preacher of whatever he did say, original or not, in order for these sayings to have been passed on. What may have been unique to him was the combination of what he said, how he said it, and to whom he said it—perhaps for this reason he has been remembered over the centuries. But one thing is absolutely certain. Whatever Jesus was reported to have said or done, it resulted in a very large, lasting change to the Western world. While we can never be certain about his sayings and deeds, we do know that his followers' feelings were strong enough to impel them to work hard, risking death, to spread his message.

So we are left to pick from the various options shrewdly. It is all too easy to select the passages about Jesus that fit the image that one is trying to build. Virtually any final picture can be formed by appropriate selectivity. You find the Jesus whom you seek. I originally did not have a specific image; I only wanted to learn about Jesus. It was after reading the books of the Jesus Seminar, Geza Vermes, and others that I formed an image. Selecting references to use introduced a bias. I then compounded my bias by considering only some of the sayings. But I believe that I have constructed a picture of Jesus that that is useful for Unitarian Universalists.

....
5   He was raised Catholic to escape the Nazis and thus has a rare dual insight into the gospels.

Where did the collections of sayings come from? There is zero evidence that anything was written down during Jesus' lifetime. He and at least most of his followers were quite likely illiterate. Virtually his entire ministry was in the rural areas of Galilee, where few could write. It is possible that he attracted a few members of the scribal class who could have "taken notes," but this is only conjecture. Probably a written version of the sayings in the form of Q came within ten years after his death, as the newly formed Jesus cults grew in urban areas. Here we are faced with the oral tradition problem. Probably everyone has played the "telephone game," where a message is whispered from person to person. Seldom is the final version even similar to the original. We can suppose that Jesus frequently repeated the same message, using similar, but not necessarily identical, words as he traveled from village to village. He probably varied the story from time to time. Thus, the followers who traveled with him could easily have learned the essence of what he said.

To illustrate the oral problem, consider this. Who said, "Blood, sweat, and tears"? Don't peek at the next paragraph until you have answered!

. . . .

If you said, "Someone misquoting Winston Churchill," congratulations! If you said, "Churchill," you have just shown how the essence of what was said is well remembered in the oral tradition but the exact words are not. (He actually said, "I have nothing to offer but blood, toil, tears and sweat.") We always need to keep in mind that we are hearing a gist of an idea and not anything literal.

Readers interested in details on the reliability of the oral tradition may refer to John Dominic Crossan, who has devoted four chapters to the subject [Crossan 1998 chs 3–6]. Rodney Stark, making a case that an oral tradition can be rather accurate, refers to the Hindu Vedic scriptures. These words were not written down until the British colonial period in India, but remarkably, the wordings gathered from distant places were similar. He notes that the scriptures endured orally for about 3,000 years with little change [Stark 2007 p 216]. On the other hand, there are cases in the oral tradition where incorrect information enters and takes on a life of its own to the point that it seems "factual." One example is in the story of Adam and Eve. Everyone "knows" that they ate the "forbidden apple." However, there is absolutely no basis for saying that the fruit was an apple!

OTHER SOURCES

We can then turn to archeology, anthropological sociology, and a general understanding of the time and place of Jesus' life. John Dominic Crossan goes into the sociological and anthropological issues in great detail in his books *The Historical Jesus, The Birth of Christianity,* and, with Jonathan Reed, *Excavating Jesus.* James Tabor covers some of this material in his book *The Jesus Dynasty.*

Archeological excavations in the Palestine area have helped our understanding of the times. For example, several of the towns and cities in Galilee have been at least partially excavated. So far, there is no definite evidence that there were any dedicated buildings serving as synagogues in Galilee in the first third of the first century. The word "synagogue" literally means an assembly or bringing together, so a synagogue of that time was likely just a gathering in a non-dedicated space in the town. One important excavation is that of Sepphoris, mentioned in chapter 1. However, this research reveals relatively little specifically about Jesus.

I will not go into detail about the excavations here but only list a few intriguing points. A stone bearing an inscription of Pilate's name has been found, adding to the historicity of that man. The question of the burial of Jesus has been controversial. Most victims of crucifixion were not buried: the bodies were either left on the cross to be picked by carrion birds, or thrown into a lime pit to decompose. Only one unambiguous burial of a crucified person has been found.

The controversial "James Ossuary" has an inscription that may relate to Jesus: it may say "James son of Joseph brother of Jesus." Many specialists think that the inscription is genuine. Despite a court decision declaring it a forgery, the question of the authenticity of this inscription has still not been settled, and the latest evidence favors authenticity. New, controversial information is still emerging.

Then there is the even more controversial "Jesus Family Tomb," uncovered in 1980 during construction near Jerusalem. It contained a cluster of ossuaries that had some names associated with names in Jesus' family. Initially dismissed, since they were all common names of the time, this collection of names is now thought by some to be unlikely to be by chance. Even the transcription of the names that are inscribed on the ossuaries is disputed. A book by Simcha Jacobovici and Charles Pellegrino, *The Jesus Family Tomb*, discusses the finding in detail. Nothing is settled as of this writing.

Even more recently, attention has turned to the "Gabriel's Revelation" tablet. The style of this unusual example of ancient writing—written in ink on a piece of stone—and a chemical analysis indicates a date from the late first century BCE. It is now hard to read some of the writing, and the exact wording is much debated. However, the text may refer to the story of a "suffering messiah" who was raised from the dead after three days. If this tablet and its message are authenticated, they will constitute further documentation of a story of a resurrected hero existing before the time that the gospels were written. This point is quite relevant for chapter 9. One problem with this tablet is its lack of provenance: its current owner acquired it from a dealer in Jordan. No one knows even where it was found: around the Dead Sea is only a guess.

Chapter 3:
Who Was Yeshua?

GENERALLY ACCEPTED FACTS

Very little is known with certainty about the life of Jesus. The only facts that absolutely no one disputes are:

Number one: Countless books written in English have the name "Jesus" in them, including the Bible and the Qur'an.

Number two: There is no number two.

So who was he?

First, his name. It is time to meet Yeshua. This was probably his name in Aramaic, derived from the Hebrew name Joshua. It became corrupted to "Jesus" through two bad transliterations. The first was to Greek, where it became "Iesous," since Greek does not have the "sh" sound. The final s was added to the name because Greek masculine names often ended in *s* (though it is not pronounced in direct conversation). Then the name came to classical Latin as "Iesus." Later, in Ecclesiastical Latin, J was used instead of the I to make Jesus, or in direct address, Jesu. The J was still pronounced with a "y" sound. English then picked up the J but not the Latin pronunciation.

Because of my negative association of "Jesus" with trinitarian theology, and for historical accuracy as well, I will start calling the historical man Yeshua (but will use "Jesus" to refer to the birth and post-Easter stories, and in direct quotes). The exact pronunciation is not certain, since we can only try to reconstruct what ancient Aramaic sounded like. But it probably was on the order of "Ye-SHU-ah," with *e* and *u* pronounced as in "met" and "true," respectively. Some suggest that the final "ah" sound should be a bit more like the German "ach" but a bit softer. However, many Americans pronounce it "YE-shu-ah." There was nothing special about the name Yeshua, which means "salvation";

perhaps 5 to 10 percent of the men at that time were given that name.
John Meier gives more details about the name Yeshua [Meier vol 1 pp
205–208].

He probably had siblings. Mark [6:3] mentions brothers and sisters:
"And who are his brothers, if not James, Joses, Judas, and Simon? And
who are his sisters, if not our neighbors?" Paul is reported in Acts to
have talked about Yeshua's brothers. Because of latter traditions of the
Catholic Church, especially the belief that Mary was a perpetual virgin,
some try to explain the siblings away by saying they were half brothers and sisters from a former marriage of Joseph. However, given that
these siblings were a bit of an embarrassment for the later church, the
fact that they are mentioned at all suggests that they probably existed.
Further, Josephus explicitly mentions "James, the brother of Jesus."
There is no evidence that Yeshua was even the oldest. That assumption
appears to be based solely on the birth myth. If he had had an older
brother, then that brother would have inherited the family property (if
any) and Yeshua would have been forced out on his own, destitute,
which might explain his itinerant lifestyle.

Here are the generally accepted facts about Yeshua. Only a very few
people say that Yeshua did not exist. He was fully human. He was a Jew,
a fact that is often overlooked by mainstream Christianity. Most scholars
place his date of birth between 7 and 4 BCE. These dates depend on
clues from the gospels, which might not be reliable. Specifically, it is
claimed that Yeshua was born during the reign of Herod, who died in
4 BCE. The limit of 7 BCE is based on gospel evidence of his age when
he started his ministry, coupled with the uncertainty of how long that
lasted and when he was crucified. Since these dates and numbers are
all uncertain, we can only say he was likely born sometime in the very
late BCE period. A further discussion of the problem of his birth date is
in chapter 7.

Yeshua probably spoke little or no Hebrew or Greek, though scholars
disagree about this. Aramaic was the local language. In that time and
place Hebrew was used only for biblical passages and during worship.
We do not know if the scriptures in Galilee were read in Hebrew and
then translated, or presented only in Aramaic. We can safely assume
that Yeshua met with the others in his village for Sabbath services. The
gospels mention that he spoke (or even read scripture) in synagogues.
However, it is probably not correct to think of a synagogue back then as

a special building, since there is no evidence that such dedicated structures existed in that region during those times.

Yeshua probably could not read Hebrew or any other language. His speeches as reported in the gospels indicate that he was quite familiar with the Torah and other Jewish traditions. He undoubtedly heard at least some of the scripture read. However, most if not all, of the scripture that Yeshua allegedly quoted from the Hebrew Testament may well have been put in his mouth by the gospel writers, especially Matthew.

Because the city of Sepphoris was only about four miles away, it is possible, though not likely, that he might have found some employment there and learned a little Greek. Several scholars think that he might have preached in Greek sometimes because of the way the sayings in the Greek-language gospels flow smoothly, lacking the choppiness that often comes with a translation. But I doubt this, since he mostly spoke in small towns to the lowest classes, who would not have known any Greek. Chapter 1 discusses Sepphoris and the probable rarity of the Greek language in Galilee.

Some Greek influence was present in the region, but there is no agreement on whether Yeshua knew any of the Cynic traditions. There were some important differences between the Cynics and the followers of Yeshua. The Cynics were loners and mostly were found in cities. The early followers of Yeshua usually traveled together, often in twos or more, and mainly visited the villages. The Cynics did not invoke a divine source.

Yeshua, on the other hand, was thoroughly Jewish and firmly believed in God, whom he often called "Father," as was common at that time. It was not a new idea invoking a father-son relationship; rather, all Israelites were considered the children of God. The word "Father" is sometimes used in the gospels in its Aramaic rendition, "Abba." Much ink was wasted making the case that "Abba" was the equivalent of "Daddy," an idea that more recently has been firmly rejected. But it is a less formal and more familiar form than "Father." As a devout Jew, Yeshua would have felt it was blasphemy to relate himself to God.

Since the story of John the Baptizer is closely tied to that of Yeshua, the focus will turn to him now. According to most authorities, Yeshua was almost certainly baptized by him and probably was his follower for a while. But Burton Mack takes exception to this statement, saying that Jesus never met John and that Mark invented this story [Mack 1993 p 155]. Robert Price does not think that John the Baptizer was even an actual historical figure [Price p 102]. The fact that Paul did not mention John the Baptizer at all lends slight support to Price's view. However, I think that John the Baptizer existed, and his followers were still active at the time that the gospels were written. The early church would have wanted to suppress any reference to a rival if they could, as John's followers believed that *he* was the messiah. The gospels worked hard to minimize John the Baptizer's role, but there must have been sufficient lore about him that he could not be ignored. Still existing today is a sect of followers of John the Baptizer called Nasoreans or Mandaeans, which is Aramaic for gnostics [Price p 102]. Also, Josephus included him in his history.

The historical record of John the Baptizer is better than that of Jesus. Josephus, for example, wrote more about John than he did about Jesus. His *Jewish Antiquities* discusses how Herod Antipas, fearing that John and his followers might start a revolution, executed John the Baptizer as a preemptive move. This is echoed in a passage concerning the death of Yeshua (see the gospel of John [11:48, 50] and my chapter 9). John the Baptizer was probably executed for the reason given by Josephus— not, as the gospels report, because John had criticized Herod Antipas' marriage to Herodias. The head-on-a-platter element of the story is pure fiction. Mark's version of the death of John the Baptizer [6:16–29] appears based on a story in Esther [Price p 14]. But there was a warning for Yeshua in John's execution: be careful about calling for a change to the status quo, especially if you have a band of followers.

John the Baptizer had renounced society and withdrawn to live off the land in the region where the desert met the Jordan River. He may have earlier been an Essene or at least might have studied with them. Like the Essenes, he held that the Temple system was corrupt and that forgiveness was attained by repenting directly to God. This did an end run around the Temple, since the priests stated that sins could be forgiven only at the Temple. John the Baptizer held that people should repent of their sins first, and then be cleansed by baptism in the river. It is important to note that immersion (baptism) was not for forgiving sins. John believed that the end of the world was at hand, so everyone needed to seek this ritual.

He did not take his message to people; they had to come to him in the desert. By making people come to him, the Baptizer was saying that he was special, a step above the rest.

While John's baptisms had negative implications for the Temple system, baptism in the Jordan had political overtones as well that went back to Moses' time. Crossing the Jordan into Judea was symbolically a conquest of that country. Even just entering the river was cause for suspicion. The Romans attacked and killed several groups who either crossed the Jordan or were planning to do so.

It is not at all clear how long Yeshua stayed with John the Baptizer, if at all. According to Mark [1:12], Yeshua left immediately after his baptism; similar wording is used in Matthew and Luke. The gospel of John mentions three days, long enough for Yeshua to recruit some of John the Baptizer's followers [John 1:37–42].

According to the gospels, sometime later Yeshua started his own ministry,[1] taking his own message to the people. While both John and Yeshua held that people could directly access God without need of the priests at the Temple in Jerusalem, their messages were mostly different. John preached that one should repent because the world was going to end soon in a rather violent manner. It was a threat: repent or else! So John spoke in these terms:

> Even now the axe is aimed at the roots of the trees. So every tree not producing choice fruit gets cut down and tossed into the fire. [Matt 3:10]
> [God's] pitchfork is in his hand, and he'll make a clean sweep of his threshing floor, and gather his wheat into the granary, but the chaff he'll burn in a fire that can't be put out. [Matt 3:12]

However, many Jews, who believed that God would intervene to help free them from Rome, thought that it was not the world would that end, but only the injustice.

The following passage compares the behavior of John and Yeshua:

> Just remember, John appeared on the scene neither eating nor drinking, and they say, "He is demented." [Yeshua] came both eating and drinking, and they say, "There's a glutton and a drunk, a crony of toll collectors and sinners!" [Matt 11:18–19a]

---

1 Actually, there is no evidence to establish how soon his ministry started after, or perhaps even before, the baptism.

John was a strict ascetic, eating very little and not drinking alcohol, while Yeshua shared many meals with the common people and especially the outcasts.

John talked about the "one coming," which standard Christianity interprets as referring to Yeshua, but many scholars think that this in fact referred to God. Various passages in the gospels have John endorsing Yeshua, but these are thought to be later Christian additions. The endorsement does not seem to be solid, since in a later passage John's disciples supposedly asked of Yeshua, "Are you the one who is to come, or are we to wait for another?" [Matt 11:3]

Yeshua's message was not about a dire end of the world. It was not "repent or else," as John preached. It was about a loving, caring God, not one of retribution. It was about the present world getting better by people becoming equal. (For more about Yeshua's message, see chapters 4 and 5.) The question of whether Yeshua talked about the end of the world is quite controversial. Many hold that this was his central point, but I do not (see chapter 5), and many scholars share my opinion.

Yeshua quite likely thought of himself as being in the tradition of the Jewish prophets. Prophets were often connected to healing. Marcus Borg sees Yeshua as a Jewish mystic, since he experienced God very vividly, as did many of the prophets in the Hebrew bible [Borg 2006 p 134].

It is generally accepted that Yeshua and his followers visited many of the villages and small towns in Galilee, sometimes all together and sometimes in smaller groups. They also went to larger towns such as Capernaum, but apparently they did not visit the larger cities. They were itinerants, dependent on the hospitality of the villagers. They spoke of a new, peaceful way that they hoped would eventually displace the rule of Rome and the enormous inequalities in their society. One very important thing about Yeshua, in his capacity as a teacher and a healer, is that he accepted outcasts, often by the use of "table commensality," to use one of John Dominic Crossan's favorite phrases [Crossan 1991, for example]. This means sitting down to a shared meal. The idea of eating with the "unclean" was abhorrent to the Jews. These activities will be covered in much more detail in the following chapters.

He may have had only a brief ministry, perhaps one to three years. As noted in chapter 2, the timetables of the gospels are not chronologically reliable. Bruce Chilton thinks that it might have been as long as ten years, but I do not put much credence in his book as it reads like a historical novel, with many unsupported descriptions and dialogues.

Yeshua was crucified as a rebel by the Romans around 30 CE. His last week and death are covered in chapter 9. The present part of this book covers only his life and teachings.

WHO HE WAS NOT

Yeshua was not trying to start a new religion. If we discount later additions to the gospels, we find no mention of a new church. He made no call to be treated as a special person. His message was what was important to him.

I (and many others) feel that Yeshua would be shocked if he were to come back today and find that he was on a par with God and some vague "holy ghost." In his mind, there was a single God. He never once even hinted that anyone should pray to him. He probably would be even more shocked to find that people are told to pray to his mother to ask for forgiveness of sins ("Say five 'Hail Marys'"). And with a few hundred "saints" thrown in to pray to, he would call it all blatant polytheism!

We could say that he wanted to start a quiet revolution, which he did. It is not clear that he even wanted to reform Judaism; his intent seems rather to get people to live a better Jewish life. Wayne-Daniel Berard claims that Jesus considered himself as part of the mainstream of Jewish life and was just trying to include the outcasts within that stream [Berard p 74].

Here are some other things that Yeshua was not. Yeshua was almost certainly not born in Bethlehem, but likely in Nazareth and not on December 25. Chapter 7 gives a more complete presentation of various theories about his birthplace and time of birth.

He most likely was not a "carpenter," even though this is one of the more persistent images. Only Mark [6:2–3] stated that he was a carpenter: "[M]any who heard him were astounded and said so: 'Where's he getting this?' and 'What's the source of all this wisdom?'...This is the carpenter, isn't it?" Luke [13:55] called him a "carpenter's son." The word *tekton* in the Greek gospels probably should be translated as "someone who builds things out of wood or stone, or does construction work, possibly as a day laborer." It does not imply a highly skilled craftsman, as we now tend to classify a carpenter. The usage of *tekton* in the gospels implies that it was a very low-class job. James Tabor supports this view [Tabor pp 89–90]. Robert Price theorizes that the expression "carpenter" in Mark or "carpenter's son" may refer to an adage the scribes used when they were having difficulty with a passage of the Torah: "'There is no carpenter, nor a carpenter's son, to explain it.' In such a context, 'carpenter' is a metaphor for [someone]… skilled in expounding Scripture" [Price p 95]. Thus the lines from Mark 6:2–3 are praise for Yeshua's interpretation. Note that Luke's use of the "carpenter's son" wording lends a little more credence to Robert Price's suggestion. See John Meier [Meier vol 1 pp 278–285] for a more complete discussion of the meaning of *tekton*.

There is no evidence that Yeshua married or had any children, although these suggestions are very popular now in the media. Most likely, he was a member of the dispossessed group and was too poor to marry. On the other hand, in advocating for celibacy, Paul took pains to note how he (Paul) was celibate, yet he never mentioned that he was following a tradition of Yeshua, which would have strengthened his argument considerably. Of course, Paul does not appear to have known much at all about the life of Yeshua. In support of the idea of a possible marriage, we have this quote from John Meier: "Celibacy as a life style for the ordinary religious Jew, and especially for a teacher or rabbi, would have been unthinkable at the time of Jesus…The silence of the NT on the subject arises from the fact that the earliest traditions about Jesus simply took it for granted that Jesus was married" [Meier vol 1 p 334]. However, other biblical figures were devoted to their prophetical cause and did not marry.

Yeshua did not study mysticism in Egypt or India, although a journey to the latter is a tempting fantasy given the similarities between his teachings and those of the Buddha, which several books have noted. He was not an Essene. Some people who link him to the "Nazorean" sect, which may or may not have been associated with the Essenes, dispute this statement. However, since John the Baptizer may have studied with them, Yeshua might have been indirectly exposed to some of their ideas and practices.

He did not perform physical miracles such as changing water to wine, stilling a storm, or walking on water. However, as Marcus Borg puts it, these miracles are metaphors that have a truth beyond the facts. E. P. Sanders agrees, saying that myths have their own truthfulness

[Sanders p 114]. The issue is not whether these miracles happened, but that people in the first century CE thought that they had. I do enjoy some of the mythology, especially Christmas with its borrowings from pagan sources. Yeshua's birth, miracles, and death will be covered more completely in the final Part of this book.

It is unlikely that he spent forty days fasting in the wilderness after leaving the company of John the Baptizer. In the bible, the number forty traditionally means "a large number." For example, it rained for forty days and forty nights, the Israelites spent forty years wandering in the desert after leaving Egypt, and Moses spent forty days on Mt. Sinai. It is reasonable to suppose that after leaving John the Baptizer, Yeshua may have spent some time in contemplation, working out his own ministry. This meditation might be compared to the Buddha's sitting under a tree meditating until he was enlightened. Both stories feature temptation by an evil force. A similar story concerns the prophet Zoroaster [see Price pp 122–125 for more about the three similar temptation stories].

There is no conclusive evidence that Yeshua ever baptized anyone as part of his ministry. The gospels are mostly silent on this point. He may have performed baptisms while he was with John the Baptizer [John 3:22–26]. The gospel of John states that Yeshua did not baptize during his ministry, but rather his followers did [John 4:2]. It is safe to say that baptism was not a central part of Yeshua's message. The reasons behind its importance in the later books of the Christian Testament, and thus for the Christian church, remain unclear.

According to the Jesus Seminar and to E. P. Sanders [Sanders p 248], he never called himself the son of God, but rather "the son of Adam" (some sources translate it as "son of man"), this being, in this context, just a way of referring to himself in the third person. This expression is definitely not a religious title. This point is discussed more in the next chapter.

The use of the term "messiah" has been clouded over by the later christology. Strictly, it means an "anointed one." Many kings, priests, and prophets were anointed. Our word "christ" derives from the Greek equivalent of "messiah." Possibly Yeshua felt that he was "anointed with the heavenly spirit" but made no messianic claims. There is no firm evidence in the synoptic gospels that Yeshua ever used the title "messiah" to refer to himself.

He did not gather "twelve disciples" but had many followers, both men and women (see the End Note). The treatment of the disciples varies from gospel to gospel. Mark portrayed them as being rather clueless and not very staunch in their belief: they had to have things explained to them several times and still did not believe in some of the physical miracles, even after having witnessed them. Quite possibly this was Mark's way of repeating the message for his readers. The disciples fare better in Matthew and Luke, and they are not very important in John, who does not even give names for all of them.

. . . .

End Note

The evidence that Yeshua had many followers seems secure, but their number is not. The number twelve was possibly used because of the twelve tribes of Israel or the twelve signs of the zodiac. None of the earliest groups, such as the Q sect, mentions the names of any followers [Mack 1995 p 68]. Some names are given in the gospel of Thomas. The gospels appear to disagree about some names. On this topic I refer readers to the tremendous detail in John Meier's work [Meier vol 3 chs 25–27, especially pp 128–135]. The disagreements involve whether Levi and Matthew are the same person, whether there was one Simon or two different ones, and whether there was a follower named Thaddeus or one named Jude, son of James. John (the gospel writer) does not seem to care: he gives the names of only five people as part of "the twelve" but adds two more names of people who could be disciples, plus the unnamed "one whom Jesus loved." Some question whether Simon, Cephas, and Peter are more than one person or variations of the name of a single person [Price pp 187–190]. John Shelby Spong believes that Judas Iscariot was a made-up person; his discussion of the disciples and their names merits attention [Spong 2007 pp 38–45]. See also the discussions in E. P. Sanders [Sanders pp 121–125] and Wayne-Daniel Berard [Berard pp 28–29] about the disciples' names, especially "son of Alphaeus," which stood for "father unknown." The name Cleopas (or Clopas) [Luke 24:18] also refers to an unknown person, as in "the wife of Cleopas" [Hendricks p 64]. Cephas and Peter may not be the same person. Simon and Peter may be different people [Price p 187]. Price also notes that "Thomas" was not an ordinary proper name [Price p 189] but the Greek name of the constellation we call "Gemini," which means "twins." The Greek name Didymos[2] also means "twin." In some stories, Jesus actually had a twin brother.

I think that part of the problem of the number of followers concerns the difference between "disciples" and "apostles." Luke [6:13] wrote, "He called his *disciples* and selected *twelve* of them, whom he named *apostles*" (emphasis added).

----

2 The gospel of Thomas opens with this sentence: "These are the secret sayings that the living Jesus spoke and Didymos Judas Thomas recorded."

Luke also mentioned seventy or seventy-two followers. (Both numbers appear in different copies of Luke. The number seventy was likely taken from the story of Moses.) John [6:66–67] referred to more followers than just the "twelve." Further evidence that there were more than twelve followers comes from a passage in Mark: "Whenever he went off by himself, those close to him, together with the twelve, would ask him..." [Mark 4:10–12]. In Acts [1:21], when the disciples were looking for a replacement for Judas, Luke wrote, "So one of the men who have accompanied us during all the time that the Lord Jesus went in and out among us...one of these must become a witness with us," showing that a larger group existed early on. Paul gives a garbled list when he speaks of the alleged post-death appearances of Jesus: "he appeared to Cephas, and then to the *twelve*. Then he appeared to more than 500 brothers and sisters...Then he appeared to James, then to all the *apostles*" [1 Cor 15:5–6, emphasis added]. Note that Cephas (who may be the same as Peter) seems not to have been counted as part of "the twelve," and that the apostles seem to be different from "the twelve."

Numerous statements in the bible show that many of Yeshua's followers were women.

None of Yeshua's brothers was stated to be a disciple, although some of them, especially James, became active in the movement after the death of Yeshua. It is intriguing to speculate that Yeshua's brother James might have been a disciple. A disciple was called "James son of Alphaeus [father unknown]" in the gospels, rather than possibly "son of Joseph," in keeping with the later church's denial that Yeshua had siblings. Certainly, James stepped very quickly into a leadership role after Yeshua's death, which would be difficult to understand, were he not a close follower of Yeshua. James Tabor goes even farther to state that not only James but also the brothers Jude and Simon were disciples [Tabor pp 164–165], arguing implicitly that Simon and Peter were different people.

To further complicate the disciple issue, the reports of how they were recruited to be followers varies from gospel to gospel, sometimes greatly so. This inconsistency casts further doubt on the validity of the "twelve" as anything from history. Followers, yes—but "the twelve," no.

Chapter 4:
Sayings and Deeds

INTRODUCTION TO THE SAYINGS

As chapter 2 makes clear, it is difficult to obtain information about Yeshua. Like many of the scholars I have cited, I think that a valid core of information remains in his sayings after the christology is stripped away. We can learn much about Yeshua by listening to his words. In fact, I think that they are the best source of understanding. We also can learn from his actions. Knowing about the general times helps somewhat (see chapter 1).

Yeshua and his followers took their message to the people, primarily in the rural villages of Galilee. This action was actually part of their message of equality. When teachers stay in one place, they are saying that they are so important that others must come to them. If anything, Yeshua was saying the opposite: you are so important that I am coming to you. Chapter 3 mentions that John the Baptizer stayed out in the desert by the Jordan River, making people come to him. The Temple system was not at all egalitarian: a person had to go to the priests in Jerusalem.

Yeshua preached that a change for the better was coming or had even begun. He spoke out against the established system of inequality, injustice, and rule by the privileged classes. His hope was that the badly oppressed lowest class would become equal with everyone else. Such equality would require that the wealthy share their resources with the poor. It was, and still is, folly to think that everyone can "have it all." A leveling requires that the high places be used to fill the lows. "The last will be first and the first last" [Matt 20:16] suggests a role reversal, but Yeshua advocated only for equality. Yeshua held that the first step toward equality was for the poor to help each other. He called his new order the "Kingdom of God" (or several equivalent variations). This term is the subject of the next chapter, where more sayings will be examined.

Yeshua often spoke in parables.[1] This form of speech was almost unique to Yeshua; it rarely appears in any other place in the bible. Gary Porton counts only five parables in the entire Hebrew Testament [Levine et al. eds p 206]. So it is reasonable to consider the parables as likely candidates for the status of authentic sayings of Yeshua. Traditionally, parables were held to have a single message. More recently, scholars view them as having an open-ended meaning. I agree.

The book *Listening to the Parables of Jesus* [Beutner ed] provides extensive discussion of Yeshua's parables; see especially the chapters by Bernard Scott, Paul Verhoeven, Robert Miller, and Robert Funk. The parables are often found in more than one gospel; however, several are unique to the gospel of Luke. One problem with interpreting them is that each of a parable's appearances in the gospels has a somewhat different wording and context. Of course, any context of the sayings and actions is suspect anyway (see chapter 2).

Parables usually aim to increase understanding. However, Mark claimed just the opposite: parables were to hide the meaning! For example,

> Whenever he went off by himself, those close to him, together with the twelve, would ask him about the parables. And he would say to them: "You have been given the secret of God's imperial rule; but to those outside everything is presented in parables, so that they may look with eyes wide open but never quite see, and may listen with ears attuned but never quite understand; otherwise they might turn around and find forgiveness. [Mark 4:10–12]

These words, which are so contrary to Yeshua's wish for people to understand and change their ways, are the work of Mark and are not authentic. What Mark might have meant by these words is puzzling. A likely explanation is that he was influenced by the secrecy of the Greek mystery cults and really meant that only a select few would be saved.

----

1 A parable is a short story that has an important message. Yeshua's parables sometimes contain an exaggeration or a shocking statement to get people to think differently.

Geza Vermes comments that Yeshua did not use the Hebrew Testament to substantiate his points, which differs markedly from the usual mode of the scribes and Pharisees [Vermes 2004 p 212]. Yeshua did not have the systematic message that a theologian would have had [Vermes 2004 p 398]. Instead, he used parables and other stories, often highly exaggerated, to emphasize his point. Marcus Borg observes that "Jesus often used the language of paradox and reversal to shatter the conventional wisdom of his time" [Borg 1994 p 80].

A study of all his alleged sayings in the gospels reveals a hodge-podge of styles and even contradictions. Obviously the gospel writers added their own creations in the name of Yeshua. I relied on two sources to help sort out the sayings. I started with the list of authentic sayings of Yeshua as determined by the Jesus Seminar [see Funk and Hoover pp 549–553 for the list and pp 16–34 for the criteria that they used]. It regards only ninety sayings as likely to have come from Yeshua. Thus, the later writers created most of the supposed sayings found in the gospels, especially those in the gospel of John. However, some of this list of ninety are fragments of a single passage in the gospels. After I put the various fragments of a single passage together, the Jesus Seminar's list amounted to only seventy sayings. In the case of sayings that appear in more than one gospel, I chose my preferred version, which of course introduces a bias.

I next relied on the judgment of Geza Vermes [2004], who worked independently of the Jesus Seminar and used his own criteria for authenticity. I compared the lists compiled by the Jesus Seminar and by Geza Vermes. Vermes held that some of the Jesus Seminar's list were not valid sayings of Yeshua, and he also held that certain valid sayings were not included by the Seminar. Sixty-one sayings were pronounced authentic by both the Jesus Seminar and Geza Vermes. Note that Vermes did not consider the sayings that are found only in Thomas. Vermes cautions that many of the proverbs and sayings attributed to Jesus are found in other sources as well [Vermes 2004 p 75]. In any event, the remarkable thing is not that there are differences, but that the Jesus Seminar and Vermes agree so much.

Precursors to some of the message of Yeshua are found in Isaiah 1:17—"Learn to do good; seek justice, rescue the oppressed, defend the orphan, plead for the widow"—and Psalm 82:3–4: "Give justice to the weak and the orphan; maintain the right of the lowly and the destitute.

Rescue the weak and needy; deliver them from the hand of the wicked."
In no way do these earlier statements weaken the message of Yeshua.

Robert Price suspects that most of the parables appearing only in
Luke are Luke's inventions [Price p 173]. He considers the gospel tradition to be not just unreliable but historically spurious [Price p 349]. I
mention Price's opinions as a caution against wholeheartedly embracing any list of sayings. However, I believe that the sayings I include in
this book are likely to reflect the message of Yeshua.

Most of the sayings validated by both the Jesus Seminar and Geza
Vermes are in this and the next chapter. By not including them all, I
am introducing another bias. See the End Note for a list of those that I
have omitted and the reasons for this. In some cases, I have used only
part of a passage in order to emphasize the particular point that I am
making.

There are explicit reasons for my exclusions. The passages I rejected
are apocalyptic, speak of a final judgment, claim a "Son of God" status,
predict a resurrection, or appear to be from the later church. Christians
will object that this removes Christ, but such an operation leaves pre-
cisely what I am trying to find: the person who is left after being di-
vorced from the christology. This is the person I call Yeshua.

Rex Weyler, in his recent book *The Jesus Sayings*, gives a compilation of sayings that he feels represents the authentic Yeshua. I do not
consider his to be an adequately independent compilation, since he uses
many of the same references that I have used. Another list of sayings,
assembled by John Dominic Crossan in *The Historical Jesus*, names 105
sayings [Crossan 1991 pp xiii–xxvi], but Crossan does not explain why
these particular sayings were chosen. He was a member of the Jesus
Seminar group, so it is not surprising that there are many similarities,
so again, we still do not have an independent list. Crossan does include
some sayings rejected by the Jesus Seminar, and all the items in his list
are free of christology.

One could go through the gospels, make a totally different selection
of sayings, and come up with a vastly different view of Jesus: not that
of Yeshua but of Christ, for example. This is what many churches do,
so that their vision of Christ dominates. I feel that they are downplaying
the message of Yeshua the person in favor of only the Christ figure. In
other words, they are focusing on the messenger rather than the message. They are entitled to their view, just as I am entitled to mine.

In many of the sayings, which are all quoted from the Scholars' Version of the gospels, Yeshua used the expression "son of Adam." Other translations use the term "son of man" or "son of humanity" or even "mortal" in these places. The usage of this term appears to have different meanings in different places in the bible. (I refer readers interested in the details to the discussion in the Jesus Seminar's *The Five Gospels* [Funk and Hoover pp 76–77].) In the quotes included here, the best meaning is often just a reference by Yeshua to himself, much as a modern person will sometimes use "this person" or "this speaker" when referring to him/herself. This was apparently a common idiom in Aramaic. Alternative meanings, such as "one," "anybody," or "everybody" are also possible in some cases. The gospel writers sometimes used "Son of Man" (with the capitals) as a title with christological implications. This usage appears to have been used only after the fall of the Temple in 70 CE [Vermes 2004 p 236]. The use in Daniel [7:13] of the term "one like a son of man" is not a title but a description, possibly referring to the Jewish people as a whole [Vermes 2004 p 236]. Karen Armstrong believes that "one like the son of man" in Daniel represents the Maccabees [Armstrong 2007 p 41].

Even though the sayings that I have selected have passed muster with the Jesus Seminar and/or Geza Vermes, some of the quotations still include phrases or words that were clearly inserted by the gospel writers. Yeshua would not have used such words as "Pharisees" and "synagogue," as these elements were not significantly present in rural Galilee during his life but rather represent the situation in the late first century. We can work around these insertions by mentally substituting them with "local religious authorities," or "local meeting place," for example. Even the degree of Yeshua's acquaintance with the priests at the Temple is questionable, since it is quite uncertain how many times he went to Jerusalem. However, questionable aspects of the sayings are acceptable when the rest of the message seems appropriate.

Please keep in mind that there are many ways to select and interpret Yeshua's sayings. I invite you to make your own interpretations, which may be quite different from mine. If you feel so inclined, please read the synoptic gospels and select your own preferred set of sayings. No one has the final word on this subject. The important thing is for you to obtain a picture of Yeshua that is comfortable for you and your beliefs. Almost any of the following sayings could be, and often is, the subject of at least a chapter. What I present here is only a brief look at some ways to interpret them.

THE SAYINGS

I will start with some of the "sermon on the mount/plain" sayings from Matthew [Matt 5:1–7:27] and Luke [Luke 6:20–49]. Matthew placed Yeshua's "sermon" on a mountain while Luke had him speaking on a plain. The two versions are parallel in many respects, though the rendition in Matthew is much longer. I note that it is very unlikely that Yeshua ever spoke for so long on so many different subjects at one time. These "sermons" are probably compilations of many sayings and parables put together by the gospel authors. The fact that some of them are found in Q and in Thomas indicates that they originally were separate sayings.

The first part of the "sermon" is often called the "beatitudes," because of the "blessed are the…" sayings in the standard translations. In the Jesus Seminar's translation, the term "congratulations" is used instead. The version of the beatitudes in Luke fits better with my image of Yeshua having a new message of hope for the lowest classes of people. (I indicate whether a saying was vetted by the Jesus Seminar, Geza Vermes, or both by the use of JS and/or GV. Q[1] indicates a saying found in the earliest layer of Q.)

> Congratulations, you poor! God's domain belongs to you. Congratulations, you hungry! You will have a feast. Congratulations, you who weep now! You will laugh. [Luke 6:20–21] JS, GV, Q[1]

Yeshua is talking directly to the lowest members of society, telling them that they are the ones to benefit from the changes he is advocating. John Dominic Crossan prefers to translate the original Greek word as "destitute" instead of "poor," emphasizing that Yeshua's message was aimed at truly dispossessed people. Yeshua was not talking about a miraculous feeding from heaven, but people helping each other by sharing.

The version in Matthew is more theologically oriented than directed at the real needs of the people.

> Congratulations to the poor *in spirit*! Heaven's domain belongs to them. Congratulations to those who grieve! They will be consoled. Congratulations to those who hunger and thirst *for justice*! They will have a feast. [Matt 5:3–4, 6, emphasis added]

I put certain terms in italics to show that Matthew focused on spiritual lacks, especially in the phrase "poor in spirit," rather than actual physical needs. However, the reference to justice does allude to the basic problem: the great inequalities that existed at that time. Note that Matthew has Yeshua talking indirectly to the people by using third-person pronouns, in contrast to the direct address in Luke. Matthew gives more "congratulations" in 5:5 and 5:7–12, but the Jesus Seminar judged these latter ones as unlikely to have come from Yeshua because they also address virtues rather than real needs.

Yeshua's message was of love for everyone.

> Love your enemies...God causes the sun to rise on both the bad and the good, and sends rain on both the just and the unjust. Tell me, if you love those who love you, why should you be commended for that? Even the toll collectors do as much, don't they? [Matt 5:44a, 45b–46] JS, GV, Q[1]

Thich Nhat Hanh wisely observes that it is impossible to love your enemies, because once you love them, they are no longer enemies! I feel that Yeshua would have agreed. Hanh's observation has a very early precedent in the Didache, Section 1:3, where it states that you would not have enemies if you loved the people who hate you [Milavec p 3]. Robert Funk said that loving your enemies was a very radical statement then (and now) [Jesus Seminar p 16].

More of the selections from the "sermons" appear in what follows, but in the context of other messages.

Besides telling the disenfranchised people that things will get better, Yeshua also spoke against the rule and abuse of power.

> You know how those who supposedly rule over foreigners lord it over them, and how their strong men tyrannize them. It's not going to be like that with you! With you, whoever wants to become great must be your servant, and whoever among you wants to be "number one" must be everybody's slave. After all, the son of Adam didn't come to be served, but to serve. [Mark 10:42b–45a] GV

The possible implication of Yeshua's claiming to have been sent by God indicates that the last sentence may be a later addition. This saying bears some similarity to a Q[1] passage.

Yeshua often called for change. The then current system of injustice, patronage, and dominance by Rome and the wealthy caused great misery (see chapter 1). Here he used analogies to explain why the old ways must change completely rather than just being modified.

> And nobody pours young wine into old wineskins, otherwise the young wine will burst the wineskins, it will gush out, and the wineskins will be destroyed. Instead, young wine must be poured into new wineskins. [Luke 5:37–38] JS, GV

This saying is linked to one about not patching old clothes with new cloth, since the new patch will shrink and rip out. Both of these sayings may have been in the common lore of the time.

> Aged wine is not poured into new wineskin, or it might spoil. [Thom 47:4b] JS

Again, the message is that you need to put the older thinking aside and not try to incorporate it into the new way of thinking.

Yeshua was of course a Jew, so following the Law (i.e., the Torah) was an overwhelming requirement. However, he was from Galilee, where traditions were looser and life was harder than in Jerusalem. It was not always possible to follow all of the provisions of the Law in Galilee. Yeshua seemed to have endorsed the Law, but at the same time he took a more relaxed or liberal interpretation. The following sayings concern the sabbath.

> The sabbath day was created for Adam and Eve, not Adam and Eve for the sabbath day. So, the son of Adam lords it even over the sabbath day. [Mark 2:27–28] JS, GV

The last sentence is a bit suspect because of the "lords it even over" wording.

> If you had only a single sheep, and it fell into a ditch on the sabbath day, wouldn't you grab on to it and pull it out? A person is worth considerably more than a sheep. So, it is permitted to do good on the sabbath day! [Matt 12:11b–12] GV
> On the sabbath day is it permitted to do good or evil, to save life or destroy it? [Mark 3:4b] GV

In other words, common sense takes precedence over blindly following the Law. The gospels report that Yeshua performed healings on the sabbath and was called to task for doing so. However, there was no prohibition on using words on the sabbath, even for healing. Most of the healings reported in the gospels involved only the use of words.

This next saying, about fasting, was considered authentic by the Jesus Seminar and Geza Vermes even though it is possibly a later addition, since it can be interpreted as a prediction of Yeshua's death. However, it shows that strict requirements for fasting were not necessary.

> The groom's friends can't fast while the groom is present, can they? So long as the groom is around, you can't expect them to fast. [Mark 2:19] JS, GV

The laws about what could not be eaten are spelled out in great detail in the Torah. Here we have a looser view.

> Listen to me, all of you, and try to understand! It's not what goes into a person from the outside that can defile; rather it's what comes out of the person that defiles. [Mark 7:14–15] JS, GV

The last part of this quote was modified by Matthew to read, "what comes out of the mouth." I like the quoted version, leaving the question of "out from where?" up to the reader. Mark later made it clear just what he meant [Mark 7:19].

> Stay at that one house, eating and drinking whatever they provide. Whenever you enter a town and they welcome you, eat whatever is set before you. [Luke 10:7a, 10:8] JS, GV, Q[1]

Again, the practical wins.

However, elsewhere in the gospels, Yeshua is quoted as saying that nothing in the Law is to be put aside, although the Jesus Seminar did not consider these passages authentic. Luke, in Acts 10 and 11, implied that after Yeshua's death his followers were still obeying the food laws.

In the Matthew sermon on the mountain, Yeshua is quoted as saying things like "Once we were told, but I tell you..." And in what followed, the injunction was usually more restrictive, often prohibiting even thoughts! For example, "We once were told, 'You are not to commit adultery.' But I tell you: Those who leer at a woman and desire her have already committed adultery in their hearts" [Matt 5:27–28]. These injunctions are not in Mark or Luke, so they are probably Matthew's invention. The Jesus Seminar voted down these passages.

So Yeshua's attitude toward the Law is ambiguous. We must also be cautious in making a firm conclusion, since the gospels were written during a time when Paul's groups were reaching out to gentiles, who did not want to follow many aspects of the Law. The gospel writers would probably have preferred to ignore issues about the Law if they thought they could get away with it, so the fact that the gospels still kept references to the Torah, in spite of the Law's lack of appeal to the gentiles, probably indicates that Yeshua did follow it. E. P. Sanders states flatly that all references to Jesus and his followers breaking the Law were inserted by the later writers to reflect practices of their own time [Sanders p 222]. Possibly Paul started the tale that Yeshua did not follow the Law when he stated, "For Christ is the end of the Law" [Rom 10:4].

Yeshua was quick to put down the establishment, especially the upper class (it was dangerous to speak out against the Romans, but as it turned out perhaps he should have been more cautious about the priests as well). He viewed the priests as hypocrites who put on a big show of propriety but were part of the system of injustice by demanding tithes and collaborating with the Romans. Because we do not actually know how well Yeshua was acquainted with the priests and Temple system, we must interpret quotes such as the following with caution. However, Yeshua must have known something about the state of affairs in Jerusalem.

> Two men went up to the temple to pray, one a Pharisee and the other a toll collector. The Pharisee stood up and prayed silently as follows; "I thank you, God, that I'm not like everybody else, thieving, unjust, adulterous, and especially not like that toll collector over there. I fast twice a week; I give tithes of everything that I acquire." But the toll collector stood off by himself and didn't even dare to look up, but struck his chest, and muttered, "God, have mercy on me, sinner that I am." Let me tell you, the second man went back to his house acquitted but the first one did not. [Luke 18:10–14a] JS, GV
> Be on guard against the scholars who like to parade around in long robes, and who love to be addressed properly in the marketplaces, and who prefer important seats in the synagogues and the best couches at banquets. [Luke 20:46] JS, GV

Probably "scholars" referred to the priests and other religious authorities. The use of "Pharisee" and "synagogue" are retrojections by Luke. In spite of these problems, I think that the underlying message likely reflects Yeshua's attitude.

In the next saying, very likely aimed at the religious authorities, he addresses those who put on an outward show but lack compassion on the inside.

Why do you wash the outside of the cup? Don't you understand that the one who made the inside is also the one who made the outside? [Thom 89:1–2 || Matt 23:25–26][2] JS, GV

Sometimes, though, he was probably referring to everyone. In the quote below, along the lines of not judging others, he observed that some people were quick to find fault with others but did not see their own, possibly larger, shortcomings.

You see the sliver in your friend's eye, but you don't see the timber in your own eye. When you take the timber out of your own eye, then you will see well enough to remove the sliver from your friend's eye. [Thom 26:1–2 || Matt 7:3–5] JS, GV, Q[1]

Yeshua could not, of course, confront the Romans or even the priestly establishment head on, so he advocated passive resistance. Obery Hendricks Jr. has this to say: "Passive resistance...is a deep commitment to changing the world around us without sacrificing any measure of our humanity...The purpose of their passive resistance was to overcome injustice without repaying evil for evil" [Hendricks pp 173 and 177]. Marcus Borg similarly observes that the way of Jesus was to practice political resistance to the existing dominating system while preaching his vision of a new life of justice [Borg 2006 p 226]. Borg then goes on to note that just following the Jewish traditions and refusing to assimilate while under non-Jewish rule was a form of passive resistance. This refusal has been generally true for the Jewish people for thousands of years.

The old revenge attitude of an "eye for an eye and a tooth for a tooth" was an important idea for its time, since it limited the degree of retaliation by saying that the damage you do in retribution should not exceed that of the original hurt. Yeshua instead said you should not seek revenge at all. Here is a crucial group of sayings for our understanding.

Don't react violently against the one who is evil: when someone slaps you on the right cheek, turn the other as well. When someone wants to sue you for your shirt, let that person have your coat along with it. Further, when anyone conscripts you for one mile, go an extra mile. [Matt 5:39–41] JS, GV, Q[1]

First, there is the explicit requirement of nonviolence. People have long debated whether this injunction prohibits self-defense. A straight reading of it would appear to do so. But the "turn the other cheek" part

---

2 The symbol "||" means that the second passage parallels the first one.

needs to be examined carefully. (I am indebted to Obery M. Hendricks [Hendricks p 169] and Marcus Borg [Borg 2006 p 249] for the following insight.) Note that the saying clearly specifies the *right* cheek.[3] According to the custom of the times, the right hand had to be used to initiate any action, since the left hand was considered unclean. Thus, for a person to strike someone's right cheek with the right hand, the back of the hand had to be used. This backhanded slap was traditionally used as a rebuke to someone of a much lower class, such as a slave. Turning the *left* cheek opened one to being slapped with the palm, which was more the way an equal was struck. Thus, the striker was forced to treat the person struck in a different, more equal, manner. It put the subordinate in charge. This saying was *not* an invitation to be battered, as it is so often interpreted.

The coat and shirt saying is quite simple. In that time and place, a person wore only those two garments. Giving up both left you naked, totally embarrassing the person suing. You won. As for the extra mile, Roman soldiers were allowed to compel a local to carry a soldier's load for one mile. But they were under strict orders to require only the single mile. So if you were conscripted to carry a load for a mile, you put yourself in charge by volunteering to go another mile. We of course have the problem that there were few Roman soldiers staying in Galilee. However, Roman roads crossed the area, so many soldiers did pass through en route from one place to another.

Yeshua took his message to the ordinary people and especially to the outcasts. It was not for the elite.

> Someone was giving a big dinner and invited many guests. At the dinner hour the host sent his slave to tell the guests: "Come, it's ready now." But one by one they all began to make excuses. The first said to him, "I just bought a farm, and I have to go and inspect it; please excuse me." And another said, "I just bought five pairs of oxen, and I'm on my way to check them out; please excuse me." And another said, "I just got married, and so I cannot attend." So the slave came back and reported these excuses to his master. Then the master of the house got angry and instructed his slave: "Quick! Go out into the streets and alleys of the town, and usher in the *poor, and crippled, the blind, and the*

3 The Didache also specifies the right cheek [Milavec p 3]. In Luke and Q[1], the particular cheek is not specified.

lame." And the slave said, "Sir, your orders have been carried out, and there is still room." And the master said to the slave, "Then go out into the roads and the country lanes, and force people to come in so my house will be filled." [Luke14:16–23, emphasis added] JS, Q[1]

Some scholars consider the above passage to mean that the message should be taken to the gentiles, especially the "go out into the roads and the country lanes" wording. But this would be an indication of an insertion from the later church, which is why Geza Vermes rejected it. I believe that instead the passage shows that Yeshua welcomed the outcasts, the destitute, and those with health problems, as in the emphasized portion of the passage.

Yeshua often sent out his followers to spread his message. Some of his sayings shed light on this by showing how Yeshua perceived the importance and strength of his message.

No one lights a lamp and covers it with a pot or puts it under a bed; rather, one puts it on a lampstand, so that those who come in can see the light. [Luke 8:16] JS, GV

A city built on a high hill and fortified cannot fail, nor can it be hidden. [Thom 32 || Matt 5:14] JS, GV

He also instructed his followers on how to travel. We can assume that Yeshua set an example by following the same rules.

[Do] not...take anything for the road, except a staff: no bread, no knapsack, no spending money, but to wear sandals and to wear no more than one shirt. [Mark 6:8–9] GV

The object of such restrictions was to show equality: the messengers were impoverished, just like those who would be listening. Earlier (as reported in Q and found in Matt 10:10), Yeshua had even said "no sandals and no staff." The lack of sandals would be a hardship, as the paths were rocky in that area. And a staff was used for defense, not just as a walking stick. So these more severe restrictions left the followers defenseless and unable to run easily. Yeshua emphasized the itinerancy for him and his followers with this saying:

Foxes have dens, and birds of the sky have nests, but the son of Adam has nowhere to rest his head. [Matt 8:20] JS, GV, Q[1]

Yeshua's first followers were likely to have been destitute already. Perhaps a little later, some of Yeshua's group had to give up what little they had to follow him. Crossan and Reed state that voluntary asceticism rather quickly replaced involuntary poverty [Crossan and Reed p 166]. Yeshua and his followers were homeless beggars. Not carrying anything made them dependent on the hospitality of the villagers. This helped to develop a network of supporters, which facilitated the spread of the movement later on. We can compare this image to some Buddhist monks, who move around carrying an empty bowl and relying on the kindness of others.

Yeshua might also have been trying to distinguish his followers from the Cynics (see chapter 1), who also went around preaching their somewhat similar message but carried some belongings with them. However, it is not certain that Yeshua was familiar with that Greek movement. We must keep in mind that it was the Greek-speaking writers of the gospels who were probably quite familiar with the Cynics.

Another series of sayings indicate that Yeshua expected his followers to be as devoted to the cause as he was.

> If they come to me and do not hate their own father and mother and wife and children and brothers and sisters—yes, even their own life—they cannot be my disciples. [Luke 14:26] JS, GV, Q[1]

It should be noted that Yeshua was mostly talking to destitute, disenfranchised people who likely had already been forced to sever family ties. The word "hate" seems too harsh. I think that "willing to leave" would have been more fitting. This saying calls into question the whole social structure of Galilee at that time, which was based on the family as the basic unit. This saying may thus be an indirect indictment of how the Roman rule was breaking apart this structure. Giving up family is of course not practical for everyone, since if there were no families and thus no children, the world would quickly end. There is no evidence that Yeshua advocated a celibate life. Certainly, there are references to some of his followers being married.

> My mother and my brothers—who are they? Here are my mother and my brothers. For whoever does the will of my Father in heaven, that's my brother and sister and mother. [Matt 12:48–50] JS, GV

Yeshua was offering instead a new community that became an extended family.

> No one who puts his hand to the plow and looks back is qualified for God's imperial rule. [Luke 9:62b] GV, Q[1]

In other words, once you start, there is no turning back.

> Follow me, and leave it to the dead to bury their own dead.
> [Matt 8:22] JS, GV, Q[1]

The above saying can be interpreted several ways. In Jewish tradition it was very important for a son to bury a deceased parent before sundown. The above saying concerns a young man who wanted to join Yeshua but felt obligated to bury his dead father first. So one level of meaning is that the new mission was more important than traditions, and there was no time for delay. I prefer to think of this saying as meaning that those who don't get the message are "dead," so they might as well just carry on as usual.

The mission was to go only to Jewish people. This is illustrated by the following three passages, which the Jesus Seminar rejected but Geza Vermes considered authentic, believing that Yeshua did not extend his ministry beyond the Jews. Since the mission was spreading to the gentiles at the time that the gospels were being written, I agree with Vermes that these passages may go back to Yeshua. Other passages, which were likely from the later church, contradict these sayings. Yeshua was not starting a new religion; he was trying to get Jews to embrace equality. It is not clear when the mission was expanded to the Samaritans, but it appears that the spread to the gentiles came later with the mission of Paul.

> Don't travel foreign roads and don't enter a Samaritan city, but
> rather go to the lost sheep of the house of Israel. [Matt 10:5b–6] GV

Some of the sayings were quite hostile to the gentiles, referring to them as "dogs" and "pigs." While this is not flattering to Yeshua, these two passages (assuming that they are authentic) do show that he saw himself as a teacher just for the Jews.

> Don't offer to dogs what is sacred, and don't throw your pearls
> to pigs, or they'll trample them and turn and tear you to shreds.
> [Matt 7:6] GV

The lack of parallelism is puzzling.

> Let the children be fed first, since it isn't good to take bread out
> of children's mouths and throw it to dogs. [Mark 7:27b] GV

In the context of this passage, "children" refers to the Israelites, and "bread" symbolizes healings.

Another possibly negative reference to the gentiles is found in the "Demons of Gerasa" story [Mark 5:1–13], in which exorcised demons are sent into a herd of pigs, which then rush to the sea and drown. Other unfavorable mentions of the gentiles in Matthew [5:47, 6:7–8a, and

18:17]⁴ may reflect a general feeling in Matthew's community, which was probably the most Jewish of the gospels writers' communities. However, the book of Matthew indicates that his group, while remaining basically Jewish, had been evicted from the synagogue. Thus they were caught between the rapidly changing Jewish traditions and the rapidly growing mission to the gentiles that had been started by Paul. Luke was more sympathetic to the "Christ movement" of Paul than was Matthew.

Some sayings remind listeners that it is never too late to join the movement and still be treated equally, and that one should diligently go after the "lost."

> For Heaven's imperial rule is like a proprietor who went out the first thing in the morning to hire workers for his vineyard. After agreeing with the workers for a silver coin a day, he sent them into his vineyard. And coming out around 9 A.M. he saw others loitering in the market place and he said to them, "You go into the vineyard too, and I'll pay you whatever is fair." So they went. Around noon he went out again, and at 3 P.M., and repeated the process. About 5 P.M. he went out and found others loitering about and says to them, "Why did you stand around here idle the whole day?" They reply, "Because no one hired us." He tells them, "You go into the vineyard as well." When evening came the owner of the vineyard tells his foreman: "Call the workers and pay them their wages starting with those hired last and ending with those hired first." Those hired at 5 P.M. came up and received a silver coin each. Those hired first approached thinking they would receive more. But they also got a silver coin apiece. They took it and began to grumble against the proprietor: "These guys hired last worked only an hour but you have made them equal to us who did most of the work during the day." In response he said to one of them, "Look, Pal, did I wrong you? You agreed with me for a silver coin, didn't you? Take your wage and get out! I intend to treat the one hired last the same way I treat you. Is there some law forbidding me to do with my money as I please? Or is your eye filled with envy because I am generous?" [Matt 20:1–15] JS, GV

4 The Jesus Seminar did not find these sayings to be authentic.

Obery Hendricks takes exception to the ""never too late" interpretation, noting that the proprietor was exploitative in that he took advantage of the labor surplus of the times and did not offer *any* of the workers a decent wage. He thus concludes that this saying should be viewed as an indictment of the economic conditions of the times [Hendricks p 133 and 137–138]. For further dissection and reinterpretation of this parable, I refer readers to essays by Paul Verhoeven and Robert J. Miller [Beutner ed pp 41–57].

Elsewhere the gospels repeat the theme of going after "the lost."

> Or again, is there any woman with ten silver coins, who if she loses one, wouldn't light a lamp and sweep the house and search carefully until she finds it? When she finds it, she invites her friends and neighbors over and says, "Celebrate with me, because I have found the silver coin I had lost." [Luke 15:8–9] JS, GV

> What do you think of this? If someone has a hundred sheep and one of them wanders off, won't that person leave the ninety-nine in the hills and go look for the one that wandered off? And if he should find it, you can bet he'll rejoice over it more than over the ninety-nine that didn't wander off. [Matt 18:12–13] JS, GV

This one is a bit of a puzzle if taken literally. Who would leave the rest of a flock unattended, to be attacked or wander off, while looking for one? Is one sheep really worth more than all the rest put together? What about equality? Aren't all people equal? Instead, it is the recruitment of another "lost" person to the movement that becomes an important occasion.

Yeshua gave this parable to show that not everyone would understand or accept his message.

> The sower went out to sow. While he was sowing, some seed fell along the path, and the birds came and ate it up. Other seed fell on rocky ground where there wasn't much soil, and it came up right away because the soil had no depth. When the sun came up it was scorched, and because it had no roots it withered. Still other seed fell among thorns, and the thorns came up and choked them. Other seed fell on good earth and started producing fruit: one part had a yield of one hundred, another a yield of sixty, and a third a yield of thirty. [Matt 13:3–8] JS, GV

The different yields possibly are to show that some people will have greater or lesser understanding. In another parable, Yeshua intimates that it might take years for the message to sink in.

> A man had a fig tree growing in his vineyard; he came looking for fruit but did not find any. So he said to the vinekeeper, "See here, for three years in a row I have come looking for fruit on this tree, and haven't found any. Cut it down. Why should it suck the nutrients out of the soil?" In response he says to him, "Let it stand, sir, one more year, until I get a chance to dig around it and work some manure. Maybe it will produce next year; but if it doesn't, we can go ahead and cut it down." [Luke 13:6–9] JS

Yeshua was criticized for spending time with the unclean and sinners (often called the "lepers" and "tax collectors"). His reply is thought to be a saying that was in general use, possibly from the Cynics, but still quite apropos:

> Since when do the able-bodied need a doctor? It's the sick who do. [Matt 9:12] JS, GV

He was not well received in his hometown. Some of the stories in the gospels are probably not authentic, but he may have been run out of his town under the threat of a stoning, thought by his family to be mad, and unable to perform healings there.

> No prophet goes without respect, except on his home turf and among his relatives and at home. [Mark 6:4] JS, GV

Yeshua had good advice about living. Some of what he said sounds like modern psychology:

> That's why I tell you: Don't fret about your life—what you're going to eat and drink—or about your body—what you are going to wear. There is more to living than food and clothing, isn't there? Take a look at the birds of the sky: they don't plant or harvest, or gather in barns. Yet your heavenly Father feeds them. You're worth more than they, aren't you? Can any of you add one hour to life by fretting about it? Why worry about clothes? Notice how the wild lilies grow: they don't slave and they never spin. Yet let me tell you, even Solomon at the height of his glory was never decked out like one of them. [Matt 6:25–29] JS, GV, Q[1]

Many of his sayings have a theme from nature, reflecting Yeshua's rural background. He found his God everywhere in nature. It is probably correct to say that all of nature, for him, was a manifestation of his God.

Forgiveness was important to Yeshua. The priestly establishment held that only God could forgive, and then only at the Temple after an appropriate sacrifice. It was considered blasphemous for an individual to forgive the sins of another. Yeshua said that we all have that ability:

Forgive, and you will be forgiven. [Luke 6:37c] JS, GV

Note the passive voice in "you will be forgiven." It is not clear by whom: perhaps by other people, perhaps by God.

And when you stand up to pray, if you are holding anything against anyone, forgive them, so your Father in heaven may forgive your misdeeds. [Mark 11:25] GV

The following saying also shows that you must forgive others to be forgiven:

This is why Heaven's imperial rule should be compared to a secular ruler who decided to settle accounts with his slaves. When the process began, this debtor was brought to him who owed ten million dollars. Since he couldn't pay it back, the ruler ordered him sold, along with his wife and children and everything he had, so he could recover his money. At this prospect, the slave fell down and groveled before him: "Be patient with me, and I'll repay every cent." Because he was compassionate, the master of that slave let him go and canceled the debt. As soon as he got out, that same fellow collared one of his fellow slaves who owed him a hundred dollars, and grabbed him by the neck and demanded: "Pay back what you owe!" His fellow slave fell down and begged him: "Be patient with me and I'll pay you back." But he wasn't interested; instead, he went out and threw him in prison until he paid the debt. When his fellow slaves realized what had happened, they were terribly distressed and went and reported to their master everything that had taken place. At that point, the master summoned him: "You wicked slave," he says to him, "Wasn't it only fair for you to treat your fellow slave with the same consideration as I treated you?" And the master was so angry he handed him over to those in charge of punishment until he paid back everything he owed. [Matt 18:23–34] JS

However, Geza Vermes states that the situation in the above parable does not reflect Jewish traditions but those of the later gentiles [Vermes 2004 p 144], since people were not imprisoned for unpaid debts in the Jewish legal system [Vermes 2004 p 91]. Also, the amount of the debt is obviously exaggerated. But the basic message of forgiving remains. It is not clear how this story has anything to do with the kingdom of God.

The "prodigal son" story may have been a creation of Luke. It is far longer than any other parable, quite contrary to the usual pithiness of other sayings.

> Once there was this man who had two sons. The younger of them said to his father, "Father, give me the share of the property that's coming to me." So he divided his resources between them. Not too many days later, the younger son got all his things together and left home for a faraway country, where he squandered his property by living extravagantly. Just when he had spent it all, a serious famine swept through that country, and he began to do without. So he went and hired himself out to one of the citizens of that country, who sent him out to his farm to feed the pigs. He longed to satisfy his hunger with the carob pods, which the pigs usually ate; but no one offered him anything. Coming to his senses he said, "Lots of my father's hired hands have more than enough to eat, while here I am dying of starvation! I'll get up and go to my father and I'll say to him, 'Father, I have sinned against heaven and affronted you; I don't deserve to be called a son of yours any longer; treat me like one of your hired hands.'" And he got up and returned to his father. But while he was still a long way off, his father caught sight of him and was moved to compassion. He went running out to him, threw his arms around his neck, and kissed him. And the son said to him, "Father, I have sinned against heaven and affronted you; I don't deserve to be called a son of yours any longer." But the father said to his slaves, "Quick! Bring out the finest robe and put it on him; put a ring on his finger and sandals on his feet. Fetch the fat calf and slaughter it; let's have a feast and celebrate, because this son of mine was dead and has come back to life; he was lost and now is found." And they started celebrating. Now his elder son was out in the field; and as he got closer to the house, he heard music and dancing.

He called one of the servant-boys over and asked what was going on. He said to him, "Your brother has come home and your father has slaughtered the fat calf, because he has him back safe and sound." But he was angry and refused to go in. So his father came out and began to plead with him. But he answered his father, "See here, all these years I have slaved for you. I never once disobeyed any of your orders; yet you never once provided me with a kid goat so I could celebrate with my friends. But when this son of yours shows up, the one who has squandered your estate with prostitutes—for him you slaughter the fat calf." But the father said to him, "My child, you are always at my side. Everything that's mine is yours. But we just had to celebrate and rejoice, because this brother of yours was dead, and has come back to life; he was lost, and now is found. [Luke 15:11–32] JS, GV

This story can be summed up as: no matter how badly one behaves, there can always be forgiveness and acceptance. However, I suspect that many of us secretly side with the angry older son, who rather correctly feels mistreated. It is hard to reconcile completely the various messages. I would be inclined to dismiss this parable if it were not for the powerful message of unconditional forgiveness.

The theme of giving and sharing is crucial to Yeshua's message. When people are in desperate need, some barely surviving and dependent on others, sharing what one has is essential. The miracle of the loaves and fish is a simple matter of sharing, along the lines of the well-known story "Stone Soup." Even today, people who have virtually nothing are often willing to share what little they have. Those who have much tend to be stingy.

Give to the one who begs from you; and don't turn away the one who tries to borrow from you. [Matt 5:42] JS, GV, Q[1]

If you have money, don't lend it at interest. Rather, give it to someone from whom you won't get it back. [Thom 95:1–2 || Matt 5:42b] JS, GV, Q[1]

Some of these sayings have precedents in the Torah (Exodus 22:25 and Deuteronomy 15:7–11, for example).

Many of Yeshua's sayings reflect the injustice of a system that permits and encourages great inequality of financial means. The solution, for those who are able, is to give willingly. The following saying

concerns a rich man who obeyed the Ten Commandments but was told
that one more action was required to follow Yeshua:

> You are missing one thing: make your move, sell whatever
> you have and give the proceeds to the poor, and you will have
> treasure in Heaven. And then you come and follow me! [Mark
> 10:21b] GV, Q[1]

Sadly, however, he kept his money and did not follow Yeshua. This
theme is repeated in this saying:

> I swear to you, it is very difficult for the rich to enter Heaven's
> domain. And again I tell you, it's easier for a camel[5] to squeeze
> through a needle's eye than for a wealthy person to get into
> God's domain. [Matt 19:23b–24] JS, GV

A person cannot be part of a system of equality while accumu-
lating wealth at the expense of the poor. If you are not a part of
the solution, you are a part of the problem. The severe asceticism
demanded by Yeshua's strict words—especially giving away all of
one's possessions—would have been welcomed by the impoverished,
who already had almost nothing and would have seen these requirements as a step toward equality.

Here are two more sayings about money and giving:

> No servant can be a slave to two masters. No doubt that slave
> will either hate one and love the other, or be devoted to one and
> disdain the other. You can't be enslaved to both God and a bank
> account. [Luke 16:13] JS, GV
> When you give to charity, don't let your left hand know what
> your right hand is doing. [Matt 6:3] JS, GV

Do your giving quietly.

Someone's giving should extend to all situations, even if it is not
convenient:

> Suppose you have a friend who comes to you in the middle of
> the night and says to you, "Friend, lend me three loaves, for
> a friend of mine on a trip has just shown up and I have noth-
> ing to offer him." And suppose you reply, "Stop bothering me.
> The door is already locked and my children and I are in bed.

---

5   Some scholars believe that "camel" is a mistranslation of the very similar word
for "rope." In either case, it is something impossible to do. The idea that the
"needle's eye" refers to a narrow gate or passage has been generally discredited.

I can't get up to give you anything." I tell you, even though you won't get up and give the friend anything out of friendship, yet you will get up and give the other whatever is needed because you'd be ashamed not to. [Luke 11:5–8] JS, GV

There is another saying that I like, even if the Jesus Seminar rated it only gray (meaning that there was only a possibility that it may have been authentic) because it is based on similar sayings from elsewhere. It concerns the idea of the relative worth of giving.

[Yeshua] looked up and observed the rich dropping their donations into the collection box. Then he noticed that a needy widow put in two small coins, and he observed: "I swear to you, this poor widow has contributed more than all of them. After all, they all made donations out of their surplus, whereas she, out of her poverty, was contributing her entire livelihood, which was everything she had. [Luke 21:1–4]

The Lord's Prayer is given in two versions in the gospels. It does not appear in Mark or John.

Our Father in the heavens, your name be revered. Impose your imperial rule, enact on earth as you have in heaven. Provide us with the bread we need for the day. Forgive our debts to the extent that we have forgiven those in debt to us. And please don't subject us to test after test but rescue us from the evil one. [Matt 6:9b–13] JS, GV, Q[1]

Father, your name be revered. Impose your imperial rule. Provide us with the bread we need day by day. Forgive our sins, since we too forgive everyone in debt to us. And please don't subject us to test after test. [Luke 11:2–4] JS, GV, Q[1]

Notably, the supplicant is asking for only a single day's food, and "debts" and "sins" are considered interchangeable.

The above quotations are the full wordings as found in the Scholars' Version of the gospels. Other versions are published in other translations. A longer version is found in the Didache, Section 8:2 [Milavec p 21]. Some Christian denominations have added wording of their own. However, according to the Jesus Seminar, only the following words are likely to have been Yeshua's:

Our Father, your name be revered. Impose your imperial rule. Provide us with the bread we need for the day. Forgive our debts to the extent that we have forgiven those in debt to us. [Matt 6:9b, 9d, 11–12] JS

A shorter version in Luke 11:2b also rated the seminar's stamp of authenticity. I give my own rewording of this prayer in chapter 6.

The "impose your imperial rule" statement is a plea for justice on earth. See the next chapter for more on the "kingdom of God." Obery Hendricks Jr. notes that the Romans may have considered calling for God to rule to be a treasonous utterance [Hendricks p 8].

The story of the Good Samaritan, found only in Luke, is well-known and was included as a likely saying by the Jesus Seminar. It appears in the context of what it means to be a good neighbor.

> There was a man going from Jerusalem down to Jericho when he fell into the hands of robbers. They stripped him, beat him up, and went off, leaving him half dead. Now by coincidence a priest was going down that road; when he caught sight of him, he went out of his way to avoid him. In the same way, when a Levite came to the place, he took one look at him and crossed the road to avoid him. But this Samaritan who was traveling that way came to where he was and was moved to pity at the sight of him. He went up to him and bandaged his wounds, pouring olive oil and wine on them. He hoisted him onto his own animal, brought him to an inn, and looked after him. The next day he took out two silver coins, which he gave to the innkeeper, and said, "Look after him, and on my way back I'll reimburse you for any extra expense you have had." [Luke 10:30–35] JS

However, Geza Vermes objects to the seminar's ruling for several reasons. The parable puts the Samaritans in a favorable light, which would have been unlikely given the general dislike of the Samaritans at that time. The dislike was mutual; a Samaritan would not have been likely to help a Judean. (On the other hand, Yeshua did like to shock people by saying the unexpected.) Moreover, a Samaritan was unlikely to have been traveling from Jerusalem to Jericho, which was not on the road to Samaria (though this could merely reflect Luke's unfamiliarity with the geography of Palestine). The actions of the priest and the Levite, who probably wanted to avoid becoming unclean by contact with blood or possibly a corpse, are consistent with the special purity rules that applied to them. But authentic or not, it still is a great lesson about helping.

I think that probably Yeshua had a parable along these lines, absent the caring traveler's Samaritan nationality and the negative view of the Jewish priests. Luke may well have heard this story and then modified it, since the church in his time was expanding its mission to include Samaritans and gentiles, and hostility to Judaism was increasing. Robert Funk devoted ten pages to this parable [Funk 1996 pp 170–180]. The story goes beyond just being a good neighbor: it says to not only help your enemies but also *let your enemies help you* (based on Funk [Jesus Seminar p 16]).

What follows is a collection of sayings that are good but do not fit easily into any category. Some are obscure in meaning but still interesting to ponder. The first, the source of a quote made popular by Abraham Lincoln, was used as an argument against those who said that Yeshua was empowered by the devil.

> Every government against itself is devastated, and a house divided against a house falls. If Satan is divided against himself—since you claim I drive out demons in Beelzebul's name—how will his domain endure?[6] [Luke 11:17–18] JS, GV
>
> Salt is good and salty—if salt becomes bland, with what will you renew it? [Mark 9:50a] JS, GV, Q[1]

Salt is used as a preservative and thus was a metaphor for purity. Salt also may have stood for wisdom. [See Weyler pp 230–234]

> As for you, be as sly as snakes and as simple as doves. [Thom 39:3 || Matt 10:16b] JS, GV

This image figures prominently as a symbol in the Transylvanian Unitarian churches. Yeshua gave these instructions to followers before sending them out on a mission. The line before it reads, "I'm sending you out like sheep to a pack of wolves" [Matt 10:16a].

> I was watching Satan fall like lightning from heaven. [Luke 10:18] JS, GV

By this, Yeshua was probably indicating that he felt progress was being made against the evil in the world.

> Give to the emperor what belongs to the emperor; give God what belongs to God. [Thom 100:2b || Mark 12:13–17] JS, GV

---

6 The version in Matthew contains the more familiar wording "every city or house divided against itself won't survive" [Matt 12:25b]. The Jesus Seminar felt that the wording in Luke was more likely to represent what Yeshua might have said.

The difficulty behind this saying is that the Torah does not prohibit the payment of taxes or tribute. Crossan and Reed note that the problem was not the paying of taxes to Caesar, but carrying Caesar's coins [Crossan and Reed p 223]. The trouble with Roman coins was that they had images of Caesar (all images of God *or people* were prohibited under the Law), and some coins even proclaimed that Caesar was god. It is often overlooked that the second part of this quote is quite subversive, from the Romans' viewpoint. It is really stating that the emperor is *not* god. Such a statement could have been considered treason by the Roman authorities.

> Grapes are not harvested from thorn trees, nor are figs gathered from thistles. [Thom 45:1a || Matt 7:16–20] JS, GV, Q[1]

The context in Matthew for this saying is about being aware of false prophets. Good things cannot come from bad sources.

I have not included the "golden rule" in the above discussion, because it appears to have been a common saying. To be sure, it is a philosophy that Yeshua did endorse, even if he was not its originator. It has been expressed in many ways, both positively and negatively. In Luke [6:31] it appears as "Treat people the way you want them to treat you," with almost identical wording in Matthew [7:12]. Mark and John did not include the golden rule.

On the other hand, in Thomas [6:3] it reads, "Don't do what you hate." Negative forms had appeared widely in previous literature. For example, in Tobit [4:15a], the admonition was, "And what you hate, do not do to anyone." The Judean Rabbi[7] Hillel, possibly a contemporary of Jesus, when challenged to explain the entire Torah while standing on one foot, was reported to have said, "What you hate, don't do to another. That's the Law in a nutshell; everything else is commentary. Go and study it." The Didache also expresses the negative form of the golden rule [Milavec p 3]. It is possible that Yeshua was the first to state it in positive terms. It is not clear whether the golden rule prohibits defending one's self or is just saying not to go on the offensive.

Besides the two ways mentioned above, there are two other alternatives. The first, another positive one, is along the lines of treating other people the way *they* want to be treated, rather than making yourself the

---

7 This use of "rabbi" here is in the sense of a teacher. The Rabbinical system as we know it today was a later development.

standard for behavior. The Jesus Seminar raised this point as an interpretation that Yeshua might have endorsed [Funk and Hoover pp 156, 476]. The final alternative is a negative one: don't treat people the way that they don't want to be treated, again making the receiver the one who sets the standard. The various ways of stating the Golden Rule are summarized in the table.

THE FOUR GOLDEN RULES			
POSITIVE STATEMENT		**NEGATIVE STATEMENT**	
You set the standard		*Treat other people the way you want them to treat you.*	*What you hate, do not do to anyone.*
	Pro	A good step toward equality. Requires helping others to have at least the basics.	Prohibits mistreatment of others, which is a step toward equality.
	Con	You might be one of those "Don't help me. I can do it myself; just leave me alone" types. Other people may have greater or special needs that you don't have.	Does not require any action to do things for others. It is only a statement of what not to do. May not meet the needs of others. Permits a "me first," self-centered way of living.
The other person sets the standard		*Treat other people the way they want to be treated.*	*Don't treat other people the way that they do not want to be treated.*
	Pro	Puts other's needs first. Requires helping. Puts you in the other's shoes.	Honors others' traditions rather than trying to change them. Prohibits the "We are going to help you whether you want it or not" attitude.
	Con	Others may be greedy or feel unreasonably entitled. Could mean enabling a substance abuser.	Does not require any action to do anything for others.
The first two are the statements found in the bible. All of the forms imply not attacking others. The question of self-defense is open.			

One can find good things and problems with all of the statements. "What you hate, don't do to another," is only an instruction not to act. Thus, no one is obligated to meet another person's needs, even basic ones such as food and water. "Treat them as you want to be treated" may not meet the needs of others who have special needs that you don't have, and it allows people who are self sufficient or want to be left alone to feel no obligation to help others. The problem of treating others as they want to be treated is that this could be interpreted as enabling all manner of self-destructive behavior. The final version, not treating others as they don't wish to be treated, again requires no positive actions.

I propose a "fifth golden rule": treat every person with justice, compassion, acceptance, and dignity.[8] In other words, consider their needs, their wants, and what they don't want. Then act with fairness and generosity.

I admit that I have been selective in the above sayings, and that my image of Yeshua has probably influenced the selection. To counteract this bias, here is a saying that does not fit the image I am building.

> Ask—it'll be given to you; seek—you'll find; knock—it'll be opened for you. Rest assured: everyone who asks receives; everyone who seeks finds; and for the one who knocks it is opened. Who among you would hand his son a stone when it's bread he's asking for? Again, who would hand him a snake when it's fish he's asking for? Of course no one would! So if you, shiftless as you are, know how to give your children good gifts, isn't it much more likely that your Father in the heavens will give good things to those who ask him? [Matt 7:7–11] JS, GV, Q[1]

It really is not as simple as just asking. Many through the ages have asked in vain. It takes positive action to change an unjust system. Wishing (i.e., "just asking") won't do it. The part about "everyone who asks receives" perhaps should be interpreted as a metaphor for spiritual asking and receiving. On the other hand, the first sentence could easily be looked at as Yeshua's "pep talk" to his followers, who went door to door until they found a receptive host. On the negative side, the first two sentences may be the origin of some of the evangelical megachurches' "gospel of prosperity," which is overtly contrary to the true message of Yeshua. Also, the word "shiftless" is not in keeping with Yeshua's compassion for the poor.

I rejected other sayings vetted by the Jesus Seminar and/or Geza Vermes because they are contrary to the Yeshua that I have found, or too eschatological, or seem to me to be from the later church (see the Endnote).

In closing this section about Yeshua's sayings, I want to stress that what is crucial is to act on the sayings, not just repeat them. The passage from Matthew [25:35–36, 40b] (see the present book's Introduction) about doing things for "the most inconspicuous members of my family,"

---

8 Sharp-eyed Unitarian Universalists will recognize that I have been influenced to large degree by the Unitarian Universalist statement of principles.

while not considered an authentic saying, very strongly emphasizes this point for me. Another quote, also not considered authentic, is along the same lines: "Why do you call me Master, Master, and not do what I tell you?" [Luke 6:46].

When we look at Yeshua's sayings, we find keen insights into people and a firm grounding in nature. It is reasonable to say that Yeshua found his God everywhere and in every part of nature. It is likely that he did not think that God worked miracles—instead, he considered *everything* that happened to be a miracle of God. Since many of his sayings invoke images from nature and the rural life that he grew up in, no special education or even literacy need be sought to explain where he got his ideas. They derived from the miracle of nature.

WHAT HE DID

Increasing our understanding of Yeshua by looking at his specific actions poses a challenge, since there is little concrete evidence of his deeds apart from the many myths about healings, miracles, and so on. We can safely say that there is no chronology of his life, except for his baptism near the start of his ministry and the final trip to Jerusalem. The Jesus Seminar considered what Yeshua might have done in its companion book, *The Acts of Jesus*. The Seminar catalogued 176 independent actions but thought that only 29 of them represented likely happenings. Some of these are as inconsequential as "Then they come to Capernaum" [Mark 1:21]. Or, "with a huge crowd gathered around him, he started teaching" [Mark 2:13b]. Some of the "acts" are just settings for the supposed miracles. There is no evidence that Yeshua performed any baptisms during his mission.

I discussed Yeshua's interaction with John the Baptizer in chapter 3. It is safe to say that he was baptized by John, because this was something that the later church would have liked to ignore but couldn't, evidently because the incident was too well-known.

To me, the most outstanding deeds of Yeshua were not specific incidents, but rather general actions, such as his going out to the people with his message and his associations with the outcasts from society. People could become temporarily unclean by doing certain necessary things, such as burying a family member or coming in contact with blood. In these cases, they could follow prescribed rules to become clean again.

Yeshua chose to be with people who were chronically unclean and cast out from society. Some were sufferers of various diseases ("leprosy" in the gospels), who were unclean until cured (which seldom happened). Some were "sinners"—deliberate violators of the Law—whom the gospels often lump together as "toll collectors and prostitutes." Beggars, who often had a physical disability, were also cast out from society. Widows and orphans were marginalized.

Yeshua served as a voice for the voiceless. Yeshua not only associated with these people; he had meals with them. Society considered people who associated with outcasts, especially eating with them or touching them, to be unclean themselves. The gospels mention people seeking to be cured just by touching Yeshua's robe. Even minor contact such as this led to uncleanliness, according to the Law.

Yeshua was known as a healer. Many of the passages in Mark concern healings. Here is the crux of his healings: *Yeshua openly accepted the outcasts and reaffirmed their humanity. He touched the untouchables, both literally and figuratively.* Chapter 8 furnishes a more complete discussion and interpretation.

The story in Luke [2:41–49] about Yeshua's staying behind at the Temple at age twelve is an invention of Luke. Nothing is known about his early life or his education, if he had any. The passage in Luke states that Yeshua's family regularly went to Jerusalem for Passover. This is interesting, since other places in the synoptic gospels imply that Yeshua made only one trip there, toward the end of his life. The gospel of John mentions three trips to Jerusalem during Yeshua's ministry, not just the one. John seems to have a different source for the traditions of Yeshua's life, which some authorities think might be more accurate. This is especially true for the details of his final days.

The subject of the number of trips to Jerusalem concerns the length of Yeshua's ministry. We can safely say that it was at least one year. The story in John implies over two years, The question of the length of his ministry is hard to answer. It depends in part on when John the Baptizer was active, when he was executed, and when Yeshua was executed. The accounts in the gospels and in the histories of Josephus contradict each other. If Josephus is correct in giving a later date for the death of John the Baptizer, then Yeshua might have had a longer ministry. Josephus, however, was not known for his accuracy. However, we also know that Luke, where we find the more traditional timing, wasn't either!

Bruce Chilton claims, without much support, that Yeshua's ministry lasted about ten years. However, as I stated in chapter 3, Chilton's book reads more like a historical novel than a scholarly work. I speculate that it must have taken Yeshua several years to cover so much territory and preach enough for his sayings to become firmly fixed in the minds of his followers. John Shelby Spong [2007] suggests that in the synoptic gospels, the duration of one year was established to fit into a single liturgical year of the emerging church, and thus should not be taken literally.

Yeshua's most controversial act was the scene where he "went into the Temple and began chasing the vendors and shoppers out of the Temple area, and he turned the bankers' tables upside down, along with the chairs of the pigeon merchants and he wouldn't even let anyone carry a container through the Temple area" [Mark 11:15–16 || Matt 21:12–13 || Luke 19:45–46 || John 2:13–16]. The Jesus Seminar believes that something along these lines happened.

It is likely that Yeshua regarded the Temple system as part of the system of inequality, so the "cleansing" story may be a metaphor for his attitude toward the priestly class, who were collaborators with the Romans. Another line of thought, developed by Keith Akers, is that Yeshua was really protesting the animal sacrifices at the Temple [Akers ch 9]; however, Akers' aim is to prove that Yeshua was a vegetarian. Yeshua held that receiving forgiveness did not depend on such sacrifices. In Matthew 9:13, echoing Hosea 6:6, we find, "For I [God speaking] desire steadfast love and not sacrifice, the knowledge of God rather than burnt offerings." There is a similar passage in Isaiah [1:11]: "What to me is the multitude of your sacrifices? says the Lord; I have had enough of burnt offerings of rams and the fat of fed beasts; I do not delight in the blood of bulls, or of lambs, or of goats."

Finally, we observe that in the gospel of John [2:13–16] the Temple-cleansing act was two years before Yeshua's final trip to Jerusalem and brought no adverse reaction at that time.

Most scholars think that some sort of a disturbance at the Temple led to Yeshua's death, though it is difficult to make more than an educated guess. The first thing to note is the enormous size of the Temple. Its area was around 24 acres, divided into various sections. The innermost was the Holy of Holies, into which only high priests could go. Then there was a larger section for the Jews. The outermost courtyard was a still larger area where gentiles were allowed.

This courtyard was also where the moneychangers and the animal merchants set up shop. They fulfilled necessary functions. The Temple tax had to be paid in a standard coinage. Pilgrims came from many countries for major festivals like Passover, bringing coins of many lands (some maybe having images of people) that needed to be changed into the standard coins. And it was not practical to bring sacrificial animals on long journeys that could last many days. So Yeshua's act was not a case of cleansing a "hideout for crooks" [Mark 11:17b].[9]

Because of the large size of the outer court, it would have been impossible to make more than a very minor disturbance: Yeshua certainly not have closed down the whole operation as Matthew stated [Matt 21:12]. If he had caused more than a very small disturbance, he would have been immediately arrested and executed by the Romans. Some people interpret the imputed action as the symbolic destruction of the Temple [Crossan and Reed p 263]. This interpretation would not have been possible in Yeshua's time, for the Temple seemed indestructible; however, the gospels were written after the Temple was destroyed. Yeshua felt that the Temple was not needed for a relation with God. Obery Hendricks states that Yeshua was trying to remove the mystique of the Temple and to say that it was not the house of God [Hendricks p 123].

According to the synoptics, Yeshua went back to the Temple over the next several days, teaching and answering questions. This return would hardly have been likely if the ruckus described in the gospels had actually happened. Had he caused a disturbance in the Temple and eluded immediate capture, he would certainly have been arrested when he returned the next day. I view the entire Temple story as a metaphorical attack on the inequality of the Temple and the priesthood, not as something that occurred. Yeshua's return to the Temple was used by Mark and copied by Matthew and Luke as an opportunity for presenting more parables and teachings. Mark had no idea of when any saying was spoken, so he could place them anywhere in the chronology that suited his needs.

But this leaves us with the question of what action caused his arrest. It certainly had to be something the Romans interpreted as potential rebellion for them to use crucifixion, since that form of the death penalty

---

9 This wording originally came from Jeremiah 7:11. Such quoting from the Hebrew Testament is cause for suspicion about the authenticity of a scene.

was reserved for high crimes against Rome. One suggestion points to Yeshua's use of the phrase "kingdom of God" and the Romans' view that any use of "kingdom" not referring to Rome was treason. It is also possible that the priests felt Yeshua was a threat to their authority. Since they were collaborators with the Romans, a simple word would have been enough for the Romans to condemn him. I discuss his arrest again in chapter 9.

Many of Yeshua's deeds, as reported in the gospels, concern his miracles. In my opinion these should be regarded as metaphors and myths, with the exception of some of the healings and the feeding of the multitudes. The gospel writers devote a large portion of their stories about Yeshua to his final week. The last Part of this book features a discussion of these topics.

So there is relatively little that we can learn about Yeshua from what he was reported to have done. That is why I have spent so much time on his sayings.

. . . .

End Note
Sayings Not Used

Eighteen sayings that were pronounced authentic by the Jesus Seminar and/or Geza Vermes are not included in this chapter or the next. Here I list them along with the reasons that I did not include them. The first block has sayings accepted by both, the second block consists of sayings accepted by only the Jesus Seminar, and the last block was considered authentic by Geza Vermes only.

Block 1—Accepted by both Jesus Seminar and Vermes

Luke 11:24–26 appears to be contrary to the idea of "healing" by removing the evil, since the cure was impermanent.

Luke 12:6–7 is a rather obvious statement that does nothing for my understanding.

Luke 12:16–20 is too eschatological.

Luke 13:24 is contrary to the idea that all can enter into this wonderful new world.

Luke 17:33 seems to have been added by the later church when there were more persecutions.

Mark 4:26–29 is also too eschatological.

Thom 41:1–2 || Matt 25:29 || Luke 19:26 is contrary to the message that the poor will be better off.

Thom 78:1–2 || Matt 11:7–8 would appear to be a reference to John the Baptizer.

Block 2—Accepted by only the Jesus Seminar

Luke 16:1–8a is contrary to Jewish practices of the time, so I agree with Vermes that this appears to be a later addition.

Luke 19:13, 15–24 seems contrary to the message of Yeshua.

Matt 5:25–26 is contrary to Jewish practices of the time.

Thom 65:1–7 || Mark 12:1–8 seems to be an allegory about "Jesus as the Son of God."

Thom 97:1–4 was not considered by Vermes, since it is only in Thomas. I simply do not understand this one.

Thom 98:1–3 was also not considered by Vermes, since it is only in Thomas. This passage is so contrary to the "love your enemy" principle that I have difficulty thinking this is something that Yeshua would have said.

Block 3—Accepted only by Vermes

Mark 5:34b does not add anything new to the ones that I have included.

Mark 9:23b goes overboard on the power of trust.

Mark 9:37 seems to imply that Yeshua was "sent" by God.

Mark 9:43–47 is too violent for me.

Chapter 5:
The "Kingdom of God"

Many translations of the gospels make frequent use of the term "Kingdom of God." The Scholars' Version uses a variety of expressions: "God's imperial rule," "God's domain," "heaven's imperial rule," "heaven's domain," and "the Father's imperial rule." Still others translate it as "God's reign" or "God's reigning" [Robinson p 198]. "Father" is used in Thomas. Matthew, who was most likely Jewish, probably used "heaven" because of the Jewish injunction against using the name of God, even in such a context. It was his usage of the word "heaven" that probably led to the idea that this kingdom was not to be on earth, although Paul also states in some of his letters that it was to be in heaven. The notion of a "kingdom of God" is rarely found outside of the synoptic gospels. The gospel of John mentions the "kingdom of God" in only one passage, and Paul called it by that name only a few times.

The expression "kingdom of God" is nowhere actually defined in the gospels, making what, where, and when it would be open to interpretation. Yeshua may have felt that the meaning was evident from his context. In any event, it would have been difficult to define explicitly, so we are left to decide what this term means to us, filtering the context through our own biases and preconceived notions. John P. Meier devotes three chapters covering 271 pages, including 592 footnotes, to the "Kingdom of God" [Meier vol 2 chs 14–16]. Meier observes that "the kingdom of God does not have a definition; it tells a story. The mythic story evoked by the phrase 'the kingdom of God' stretches from the first page of the bible to its last, and a given context will highlight one aspect of the multifaceted symbol rather than another" [Meier vol 2 p 241].

I will eventually give my own interpretation of the term "Kingdom of God" in chapter 6. For now, to avoid the gender-biased term "kingdom" and to give a hint of my own interpretation, I will use "dominion of justice," except when quoting.

Two words that are often used in conjunction with the possible coming changes in the world have different meanings depending on who is using them: "apocalypse" and "eschatology" (and their adjectival forms). Strictly speaking, an apocalypse is a revelation. It quite frequently means a revelation of a violent end to the world, often as divine retribution for the world's sins. Eschatology literally means "speaking about the end of times." It can mean the end of a present system, leaving open the possibility of a new order replacing current affairs rather than the world actually ending. Marcus Borg views eschatology as an ideal state of things yet to come. Violence is not necessarily implied by eschatology. To confuse things still more, a variety of adjectives can further delineate eschatology: ethical, realized, imminent, future, and even apocalyptic. John Dominic Crossan discusses the various meanings at some length [Crossan 1998 pp 257–271]. He particularly favors "ethical eschatology" when speaking of his understanding of Yeshua's new order.

So how will these terms be used in the rest of this book? For me, "apocalypse" means a final judgment with a violent end to the world. "Eschatology" means an end to the present order to be replaced by a better one.

The Hebrew Testament refers to a better world coming here on earth. For example, Isaiah 2:4 foretells that "[God] shall judge between nations, and shall arbitrate for many peoples; they shall beat their swords into plowshares, and their spears into pruning hooks; nation shall not lift up sword against nation, neither shall they learn war anymore." Micah 4:3 echoes some of the passage of Isaiah, adding "But they shall all sit under their own vines and under their own fig trees, and no one shall make them afraid" [4:4]. In Amos 9:14 we find, "I [God speaking] will restore the fortunes of my people Israel, and they shall rebuild the ruined cities and inhabit them; they shall plant vineyards and drink their wine, and they shall make gardens and eat their fruit."

On the other hand, John the Baptizer was clearly calling for a fiery apocalyptic end of the world to happen soon, so it was "repent or else." Recall the following statements from chapter 3:

> Even now the axe is aimed at the roots of the trees. So every tree not producing choice fruit gets cut down and tossed into the fire. [Matt 3:10]

[God's] pitchfork is in his hand, and he'll make a clean sweep
of his threshing floor, and gather his wheat into the granary, but
the chaff he'll burn in a fire that can't be put out. [Matt 3:12]

It may be that Yeshua, realizing that people must *do* something instead of just waiting for God, changed from John's message to one of action. Indeed, this difference could have been why he left the fellowship
of John the Baptizer. Yeshua was calling for a new world order here on
earth, not predicting the destruction of the earth or a final judgment as
a threat to get people to behave properly. For him, doing good things for
people was something that one should do because it is the just and the
proper thing to do. He was for action, not a passive waiting for the end.

Yeshua, of course, lived under Roman rule and the vast inequalities
that an imperial system of domination creates. The dominion of justice
was placed in direct opposition to the Roman domination. While Yeshua
never said this in direct words, his many calls for equality point in that
direction.

Where will this dominion of justice be located? This question has
been asked since the time of the gospels. It is unclear whether the early
church thought that this dominion was to be here on earth or literally
"in heaven." I feel that Yeshua was talking about something on earth.
One thought is that a fully realized system of peace, equality, and justice
would indeed be "heaven on earth," thus combining the two positions.

The other big question was when. Was it already present, coming
soon, or perhaps in the distant future? All of these are possibilities in
the Christian Testament. The answer depends in part on which passages
in the gospels are considered valid and how much weight is assigned
to the non-gospel part of the Christian Testament, especially the book
of Revelation. See the discussions in Meier, cited above, and in *The Five
Gospels* [Funk and Hoover pp 136–137].

The writings of Paul do nothing to clarify the issue, since he stated
several alternatives. Much of his writing speaks of a future event where
spiritual bodies will rise into the heavens. For example, 1 Cor 15:44a,
and 50a read "It is sown a physical body, it is raised a spiritual body...
Flesh and blood cannot inherit the kingdom of God." But he also has a
here-and-now message: "For the kingdom of God is...righteousness and
peace and joy in the Holy Spirit" [Rom 14:17].

The earliest writings in Q[1] and Thomas make no mention of a dire
end. Rather a new, better, radically different world is envisioned. People,

by their actions, will bring about the new order. Later layers in both of these sources become more apocalyptic.

Luke implied a "here on earth in the near future" view in this quote:

> Congratulations, you poor! God's domain belongs to you. Congratulations, you hungry! You will have a feast. Congratulations, you who weep now! You will laugh. [Luke 6:20–21]

I see in the words of Yeshua an advocacy for active reform here on earth. Obery Hendricks agrees strongly with this position, making the case that "in practical terms, then, Jesus' way—that is, Jesus' conception of God's kingdom—is a society based on love of others rather than self-centeredness and greed; an economy based on cooperation and consideration of others rather than cronyism; politics based on service rather than selfishness" [Hendricks p 183]. Hendricks is speaking about the situation two thousand years ago as well as about America right now.

We must look at what Yeshua had to say about the above questions. I first quote one that clearly shows a present realization.

> But if by God's finger I drive out demons, then for you God's imperial rule has arrived. [Luke 11:17–20] JS, GV

An evil spirit was thought to be the cause of many of a person's ills. Yeshua was known as an exorcist as well as a healer. Most of us do not believe in demonic possession in this day and age,[1] but people in the first century CE did. They reasoned that Yeshua must have performed exorcisms because they saw people being cured. People got better when they were accepted back into society and had their humanity reconfirmed. In the above saying, the curing of the demon called ostracism was a sign that the dominion of justice had arrived for those people.

Yeshua had a hard time explaining what his concept of the dominion of justice was, since it was such a radical change from the existing system. He relied on analogies in the following, as in so many other sayings. The next four sayings all support the idea that Yeshua thought that the dominion of justice was already present on this world, if only by a toehold. Bigger and better things were still to come.

> It will not come by watching for it. It will not be said, "Look, here!" or "Look, there!" Rather the Father's imperial rule is

---

1 However, exorcisms are still performed today. Some are even shown on TV.

> spread out upon the earth, and people don't see it. [Thom
> 113:2-4 || Luke 17:20–21] JS, GV
> Heaven's imperial rule is like a mustard seed. It is the small-
> est of all seeds, but when it falls on prepared soil, it produces
> a large plant and becomes a shelter for birds of the sky. [Thom
> 20:2–3 || Matt 13:31–32] JS, GV, Q[1]

This saying has a hidden implication, as a mustard plant is a weed
that can grow out of control to take over an entire field. Perhaps it is a
metaphor for the oppressed peasant class taking over from the wealthy
upper class that typically owned the agricultural land. Letting an absen-
tee property owner's field go to weed is a form of passive resistance.

> Heaven's imperial rule is like leaven which a woman took and
> concealed in fifty pounds of flour until it was all leavened.
> [Matt 13:33] JS, GV

And thus ready to rise. However, like many sayings, this one lends
itself to alternative interpretations. Bernard Scott [Beutner ed p 99] notes
the use of "conceal" instead of "mixing." Something is being hidden.
Leaven was considered a symbol of uncleanliness or moral evil. With
this thought in mind, we have a totally contradictory juxtaposition here.
How could a woman hiding evil possibly be related to the dominion of
justice? I am sticking with the simple interpretation that it is the start of
something good that will rise.

> I have cast fire upon the world, and look, I'm guarding it until
> it blazes. [Thom 10 || Luke 12:49] JS

I do not interpret this saying to mean a fiery or violent end of the
world. Rather, that the dominion of justice has been kindled and will
soon be more evident.

Here are some more analogies that Yeshua used to get his concept
across.

> Let the children come up to me, don't try to stop them. After
> all, God's domain is peopled with such as these. [Mark 10:14b]
> JS, GV

This coming new order will have innocent, gentle people in it. Young
children often share and feel empathy for each other. They smile readily
at everyone before they learn to be afraid of the unknown.

> Heaven's imperial rule is like treasure hidden in a field: when
> someone finds it, that person covers it up again, and out of
> sheer joy goes and sells every last possession and buys that

field. Again, Heaven's imperial rule is like some trader looking for beautiful pearls. When that merchant finds one priceless pearl, he sells everything he owns and buys it. [Matt 13:44–46] JS, GV

"Treasure" and "pearl" are clearly metaphors for the dominion of justice in the above saying. Yeshua envisioned a peaceful, just existence. This new world order was worth giving up everything. If we hark back to the previous chapter, we indeed find an admonition to sell everything and follow Yeshua, with the proceeds going to the poor. The two examples in the above quote have multiple implications. Several authors point out problems with this passage. The first sentence advocates doing something dishonest or at least immoral. According to custom, anything in or on a person's land belongs to that person. Thus, the treasure belonged to the landowner. The person who found it and re-hid it was essentially stealing it from the landowner. There is also the possible implication that the person is keeping the treasure. In both parts of the saying, the person is left with nothing that can benefit him by itself. The merchant cannot eat the pearl or live in it, for example. Both of these cases are totally contrary to the sayings of Yeshua that instruct people to sell everything and *give the proceeds to the poor*, rather than hoard wealth for themselves. I think that digging for these interpretations is taking the passage too literally. Many of Yeshua's sayings are metaphors. So I will stay with my interpretation given above.

Many scholars agree that the dominion of justice was to be on earth. Marcus Borg maintains that it was not conceived as being only in the afterlife, noting, "In short, like the Lord's Prayer, the Beatitudes confirm that the kingdom of God is both religious and political: it is *God's* kingdom, and it is a *kingdom on earth* that involves a transformation of the life for the poor and hungry" [Borg 2006 p 190, emphasis in original]. He later adds, "The kingdom of God is not about heaven...It is about a transformed world, a world of justice and plenty and peace" [Borg 2006 p 252]. Burton Mack contends that it was an earthly social vision. Obery Hendricks also observes that in most of Yeshua's statements in the gospels, the kingdom of God is an earthly reality [Hendricks p 22]. He sees Yeshua treating people and their needs as holy. "The kingdom (or sovereignty) of God was a new world order of transformed human relationships; it was social, economic, and political relationships in the world made holy" [Hendricks p 99]. Crossan and Reed state, "All that was still possible [in the time of Jesus] was to attempt the redistribution of eating and healing, of the material and spiritual bases of life, from the bottom upward. That was the Kingdom of God. On earth" [Crossan and Reed p 176].

The whole idea of the dominion of justice is that it is a relation between people, and not a relation between people and god. God is not going to give you something for which you become indebted to him. Rather, if someone does something for you, then you should do something for someone else. You do not "owe" your benefactor anything—you owe humanity, so you do a service for someone else. The dominion of justice is a chain reaction. Where does this chain start? I say that it comes from the underlying sense of goodness, love, and what is right that is part of the Universal Spirit. James Robinson puts it this way: "There is an explicit reciprocity in what Jesus has to say about God reigning: we receive from God through what he motivates other people to do for us, and other people receive from God through what he motivates us to do for them" [Robinson p 171]. It is people looking out for each other, not everyone for him or herself.

There is a real message in this for today. We need to care for other people, especially those in severe need. James Robinson has this to say, speaking about right now: "Selfishness may ultimately turn out to be a luxury we can ill afford" [Robinson p xii]. And in the interpretation of Crossan and Reed, "The Kingdom of God, in other words, was not just a vision but a program, not just an idea but a lifestyle, not just about heaven hereafter but about earth here and now, and not just about one person but about many others as well" [Crossan and Reed p 319].

According to both the Jesus Seminar [Funk and Hoover] and Geza Vermes [Vermes 2003], Yeshua never preached about an apocalyptic end of time such as the New Testament portrays in several places, including the gospels. All of the references to an apocalypse with "one like the son of man" coming on a cloud (referring to an image from the book of Daniel) are later additions. Rather, as we have seen, Yeshua did speak of the dominion of justice coming or even here. His vision was of the possibility of people living in equality, peace, and harmony on this earth. It was not an apocalypse. It was not a call for a revolution. It was a call for a radical (but peaceful) change. To paraphrase John Dominic Crossan, we can say that with an apocalypse, we are waiting for God to do it for us. But in an ethical eschatology, God is waiting for us to do something about the evil in this world [Crossan 1998 pp 283–284]. It is the latter that Yeshua was trying to do. One thing to note about the violent end of the world that some predict is that the image of widespread death and destruction is not compatible with Yeshua's God of love and kindness. His God was not a bringer of revenge but of justice.

James Robinson sets forth this meaning for the dominion of justice:

> The kingdom of God is not God's stamp of approval on the status quo, the powers that be, the ruling class. Rather, it is countercultural, for it gives hope to the hopeless. It is not consoling them with "pie in the sky by-and-by," but involves concrete intervention in the lives of the needy, mitigating their plight in the here and now [Robinson p 170].

This statement is at least as valid today as it was two thousand years ago.

John Dominic Crossan summarizes the expression "Kingdom of God" as "radical egalitarianism." Having universal equality would indeed be a radical change, not only in Roman times but here today. Walter Wink defines the same term as "God's domination-free order" [quoted in Rasor p 72], observing also that "violence is the ethos of our times…It, and not Christianity, is the real religion of America" [ibid.].

The gospels state that Yeshua's disciples and others ask, "When will this happen?" As we have seen, his words say that it has already started. (It is too bad that twenty centuries have passed and we still do not have a final actualization. When will we ever learn?) However, the Christian Testament, mostly written after the destruction of the Temple in 70 CE, adds apocalyptic messages about a second coming of Jesus "on a cloud," that will happen during the lives of the readers. Paul was especially adamant that this rather apocalyptic event would happen very soon. Unfortunately, the generations have passed with no such mystical arrival, prompting much fancy scrambling on the part of the Christian church by way of explanation.

All of these varied views complicate the interpretation of the "Kingdom of God." I will offer my own understanding of the dominion of justice in the next chapter, where I finally give my own interpretation and relate it to Unitarian Universalist principles.

Chapter 6:
Yeshua For Today

Galilee in the first century CE is distant, in space and especially time. Do Yeshua and his message belong only to this far-off time and place? Some people seem to think so. The situation now is so different in many ways, with billions more people spread over a globe that was largely unknown to ancient people. We have technologies that they could not have imagined. The economy differs vastly: agriculture, while still vital, no longer occupies 90 percent of the population. With all of these differences, can we still find meaning in Yeshua and his teachings today? This chapter's answer is a resounding "YES!"

YESHUA THROUGH THE AGES

Here is an insight about Yeshua that puts him into a more universal perspective, stretching through the ages. The so-called "second coming" has already happened many times, both before and after Yeshua's life. He can be thought of as a special reflection of the Universal Spirit that appeared earlier as the Hebrew prophets Elijah and Amos, as Lao-Tzu and the Buddha, then later as Muhammad, Jane Addams, Gandhi, Albert Schweitzer, Martin Luther King Jr., and Mother Teresa. These people acted for a better way of life. They were for changing, reforming, giving, and living in peace. I have mentioned only a few of the many possible people. Please add your own inspiring women and men to this list of "Yeshuas through the Ages."

John Dominic Crossan supports this idea.

> Lest you imagine...that I am inventing some unique theology for a unique Jesus, let me assure you that I find ethical eschatology in the nonviolent resistance to structural evil put

forward by such diverse people as Jain Mahatma Gandhi, the Catholic Dorothy Day, and the Protestant Martin Luther King, Jr. If enough people lived like *they* did—lived in nonviolent protest against systemic evil, against the normalcies of this world's discrimination, exploitation, and oppression—the result would be a new world we could hardly imagine. That is eschatology— possibly the only real type available to us. [Crossan 1998 p 279, emphasis in original]

This idea of Yeshua being in the spirit of previous individuals is not new. Robert Price notes that the Ebionites[1] held that Jesus was the latest reincarnation of prophets such as Enoch, Noah, Moses, and others [Price p 249].

A SUMMARY OF YESHUA'S MESSAGE

The highlights of Yeshua's teachings and life are a fitting lead-in to relating his message to the present time. Yeshua taught that creating the dominion of justice depended on embracing equality, rather than on sacrifices at the Temple, baptism, or even simple belief such as Paul and the later church posited. Yeshua openly accepted outcasts, destitute people, and all others who were marginalized by the establishment. His principle thrust was toward fairness and justice for all. One of his ways of working toward equality was to promote sharing among cohorts. Sharing amongst the poor is different from receiving alms from the upper class. The former is a type of equality, while the latter is giving in to the class system.

Yeshua taught that anyone can have a direct relation with the Universal Spirit. Intermediaries are not only unnecessary, but they get in the way.

It is difficult to select just a handful of Yeshua's sayings to represent his message, but I have compiled a list of his sayings that I think come close to epitomizing it.

- Don't react violently against the one who is evil: when someone slaps you on the right cheek, turn the other as well. When someone wants to sue you for your shirt, let that person have your coat along with it. Further, when anyone conscripts you for one mile, go an extra mile. [Matt 5:39–41]

....
1   The Ebionites were a Christian Jewish sect in the early centuries of the Common Era.

- Love your enemies. God causes the sun to rise on both the bad and the good, and sends rain on both the just and the unjust. [Matt 5:44, 445b]
- I swear to you, it is very difficult for the rich to enter Heaven's domain. And again I tell you, it's easier for a camel to squeeze through a needle's eye than for a wealthy person to get into God's domain. [Matt 19:23b–24]
- Give to the one who begs from you; and don't turn away the one who tries to borrow from you. [Matt 5:42]
- Congratulations, you poor! God's domain belongs to you. Congratulations, you hungry! You will have a feast. Congratulations, you who weep now! You will laugh. [Luke 6:20–21]
- That's why I tell you: Don't fret about your life—what you're going to eat and drink—or about your body—what you are going to wear. There is more to living than food and clothing, isn't there? Can any of you add one hour to life by fretting about it? [Matt 6:25, 27]
- Why do you wash the outside of the cup? Don't you understand that the one who made the inside is also the one who made the outside? [Thom 89:1–2 ‖ Matt 23:25–26]
- You see the sliver in your friend's eye, but you don't see the timber in your own eye. When you take the timber out of your own eye, then you will see well enough to remove the sliver from your friend's eye. [Thom 26:1–2 ‖ Matt 7:3–5]

Keep in mind that Yeshua often used metaphors and exaggerations, and that he was speaking about an earthly system of justice and equality. You may wish to review the discussions of these sayings in chapter 4, and perhaps add a few more of your own choosing to the above list.

There are two other sayings that I feel need to be rephrased to express my understanding of the spirit of Yeshua's message. First is a modified version of the "Lord's Prayer" that is much more compatible with my own religious outlook.

We honor the Universal Spirit.
May the dominion of justice be realized here on earth.
May everyone have enough of the necessities of life.
May we have compassion and forgiveness for all.

The other is the golden rule. In chapter 4, I proposed a modified version that covers its spirit without the drawbacks: treat others with justice, compassion, acceptance, and dignity.

Certainly, Yeshua's message and its meaning are vastly greater than the above short list. If I had to summarize his message in one word, it would be "justice." A close second choice for that single word is "equality," but I would argue that there must be justice before there can be equality. Greed and self-interest are completely contrary to Yeshua's ideals. He was against privileges and entitlement.

His sayings alone do not tell the entire story. An important part of his significance lies in what he did. He went to the poor and sick where they were, treating them with compassion and thus accepting them back into the embrace of society. Much of the illness at that time is likely to have been caused by ostracism (see chapter 8 on healings). His actions stand in vivid contrast to those of many people today, who pretend that the poor, the sick, the homeless, and the hungry simply do not exist. Some even claim that the homeless are that way by choice (it is tempting to mention a prominent name), blaming the victims of our unjust society for their problems.

Yeshua championed the common person—the lowest class of people, who were beaten down by the consequences of the Roman rule and heavily in debt. He used the idea of gathering for table fellowship in common meals as a way of reaching out to the oppressed. This table fellowship set an example of sharing what one had, pointedly including the outcasts of society.

Alongside all of the countless opinions as to who Yeshua was, I am adding my own. Yeshua was a person whose uncorrupted message I endorse. He stood for positive actions, helping other people, and sharing. I think that it is no stretch to say he was a liberal.[2] It is too bad that conservative politicians have turned "liberal" into a dirty word! Yeshua preached equality, both in life and in spiritual practices. He readily accepted women as his followers. He was a counterculturalist, an extraordinary person, a teacher, and an advocate for action to improve people's lot.

Can one find the divine in a fully human Yeshua? Of course!! The simplest statement is that there is something divine in everyone. But

2 Many others have suggested that Yeshua was a liberal. See *Jesus Was A Liberal* by Scotty McLennan, for example.

Yeshua, who saw his God everywhere and in everything, was a special person who lived in his God. He certainly was not unique in this respect; other holy people have also embodied this special reflection of the Universal Spirit. The list of "Yeshuas through the ages" at the beginning of this chapter gives just a few of the many examples.

YESHUA AND THE UNITARIAN UNIVERSALIST PRINCIPLES

I finally am giving my definition of the dominion of justice as a society where:
- People enjoy justice and equality and show compassion in human relationships.
- There is an acceptance of one another, recognizing the worth and dignity of every person.
- Peace, liberty, and justice for all are embraced.

These characteristics of the dominion of justice may have rung a bell for Unitarian Universalist readers, because they incorporate some of our Unitarian Universalist principles.

The seven principles that Unitarian Universalist congregations affirm and promote are:

1. The inherent worth and dignity of every person;
2. Justice, equity, and compassion in human relations;
3. Acceptance of one another and encouragement to spiritual growth in our congregations;
4. A free and responsible search for truth and meaning;
5. The right of conscience and the use of the democratic process within our congregations and in society at large;
6. The goal of world community with peace, liberty, and justice for all;
7. Respect for the interdependent web of all existence, of which we are a part.

Principles 1, 2, 3 (first half), and 6 fit perfectly with the teachings of Yeshua. I feel that Yeshua, who so often used analogies from nature, would have agreed with the seventh principle. He was close to the land and found the Universal Spirit everywhere in nature. The remaining principles reflect ideas that could not have been imagined in his time.

Yeshua would have been shocked at the thought of trinitarianism. To him, there was only one God. The benediction before the Shema, which he would have known and repeated, states, "Hear O Israel, the Lord our God, the Lord is one!" [Deut 6:4]. He certainly would have agreed with the rallying cry of our Unitarian Transylvanian origins: *Egy Az Isten*, God Is One. He repeatedly spoke of a single God. So Yeshua, in his actions and teachings, was totally aligned with an activist version of Unitarianism. His sayings deserve a place alongside our other sources of inspiration, rather than the neglect so often found in Unitarian Universalist churches. Yeshua would feel at home in a Unitarian Universalist church, so let's make his ideas welcome. We need to understand his teachings and act in that spirit.

YESHUA FOR TODAY

What is the relevance of Yeshua's message for us here and now? His actions, and what he said about justice and equality, are just as appropriate today as they were back then. Many people either do not believe this or pay it only lip service and go about business as usual, without actually following his teachings. People of all religious bents can embrace my understanding of Yeshua and his relevance for today, as covered in this and the next section of this chapter. They can find guidance for the problems of today in his two-millennia-old message. Christians who have focused on the Christ image to the neglect of Yeshua's message should become reacquainted with his teachings and the need to act on them now. They were not just for two thousand years ago.

A recent study shows the harm done by ignoring Yeshua's plea for equality. Richard Wilkinson and Kate Pickett, in their new book *The Spirit Level*, present extensive data to support their thesis that a root cause of many of the health and social ills in the world is *inequality* of income. Study after study support this claim. As income differences in the countries studied increased, anxiety rose, trust declined, and mental illness, drug use, infant deaths, obesity, the teenage birth rate, and the percentage of people in prison increased, to mention just some of their results. Perhaps more tellingly, they show that the absolute income level in a country is much less of an influence on these measures than is income inequality. They also look at data from different states in America that show similar trends. Thus Yeshua's call for equality finds detailed support today.

Here is a quick quiz: A great nation believes that it has the right, even the duty, to impose peace on the world by invading other nations.

It claims that the way to peace is through victory. Its political system is based on the wealthy preserving the status quo. Only a few percent of the people control the majority of the wealth. The gap between the rich and the poor continuously widens. Many people, especially those living in the countries occupied or under the influence of this one nation, live in poverty, lacking adequate food and shelter. The question is whether I am talking about the Roman Empire or the United States today.

The answer is that it really doesn't matter, as I have both in mind! Now is finally the time to replace the Roman "peace through victory," which did not work then and does not now, with "peace through justice," which just might work, if we could only let go of narrow ideologies and self-interest. Let's give peace a chance (cue in John Lennon and the Plastic Ono Band). Maybe we could then begin to realize the dominion of justice.

The situation in this country right now is similar in some ways to the situation in Roman times. We live in a society where the rich by and large are in control and becoming richer, while the poor get poorer. We are far from equality in race, gender, and economic matters. Corruption and greed exist in some of the highest places in business, government, and churches. Yet our society tolerates this. Why? What can we do? Acting on Yeshua's ideas and deeds would be a good starting place.

We are too much a nation of self-interest, and not very enlightened at that. Politicians, who often talk an enlightened message while running for office, generally give in to the special interests that helped elect them, forgetting the common people in favor of the wealthy and corporations. Much of this is the result of pressure to do what is necessary to get reelected. Whatever happened to term limits? Tax breaks for the wealthy who help finance political campaigns are prioritized over food, housing, and medical care for the poor. The health care reform that was recently passed faces fierce opposition and will probably be modified. Food costs keep going up while the small farmer gets squeezed. Serving special interests appears to be more important than the environment. I want to make clear that I am picking on both the Democrats and the Republicans who share these faults, even as I acknowledge that there exist politicians who *do* care about the poor and the environment.

Looking at this country and the world through "Yeshua eyes," we can see many situations where his principles would help. Two major events that were happening at the time that I was writing this book are especially noteworthy. First was the needless invasion of Iraq.[3] Whenever we fight an unjust war—killing many tens of thousands of unarmed men, women, and children, all on the basis of false information—something is radically wrong. Our response vastly exceeded any hurt done to us: in terms of Iraqi deaths versus American deaths, it was likely at least twenty times more severe, not to mention that Iraq had nothing to do with the terror attacks of 9/11. Even the old "eye for an eye" would not condone such a lopsided response.

Our actions, based on our black-and-white "for us or against us" attitude, have cost us almost all the respect we once had in the Middle East, and indeed, worldwide. Whatever happened to "Love your enemies"? We should be loving and helping people, not annihilating them. The job of rebuilding the country and "winning the hearts and minds of the people" was almost totally botched by mismanagement, political opposition, and corruption. As someone said, we should try to influence people not by the example of our power, but by the power of our example. Still, we must first set the good example for this to happen. Even if the unrest is over by the time you read this, the general objections remain valid. Similar comments apply to the earlier invasion of Afghanistan, with the conflict still continuing.

Another big problem while this book was being written was the blow to our economy caused, in my opinion, by greed. "Self-regulation" of the financial system turned into greedy self-interest. The attitude in many cases apparently became, "Let's get as much money as the weak legal system allows without worrying about who may get hurt." To be sure, even some of the greedy people ended up hurting when the whole misguided system collapsed like a house of cards. But common people suffered much more. Yeshua would certainly condemn the attitude of looking out for only one's narrow self-interest. "Trickle down" did not work. Instead, we should have a "bottom up" rebuilding of society, helping the poor and disadvantaged first. If the formerly poor had decent jobs, the rich would benefit from the economic boost of their increased consumption and taxes paid, as well as from reduced crime and health costs.

Besides war and an economic meltdown, we face climate change and with it, energy, food, and water shortages. People and especially

---

3 Fortunately, the Iraq situation appears to be winding down, but with an unknown religious strife that may follow.

corporations, looking for short-term gains, are behind many of these problems. Can humanity ever take a long-term selfless look at the world? Where is Yeshua's equality and caring for others? Can we be inspired by the image of the dominion of justice?

ACTING ON THE ISSUES

It is not enough to embrace principles without acting on them. Yeshua was concerned with actively challenging the existing system to improve humanity's lot. He said that acting on the message of the present and coming dominion of justice was all-important. Actions talk, words walk. And we still need to act; Yeshua's ideal is nowhere near realization. This action theme shows up many places in the gospels. An outstanding one is from part of Matthew 25 (a shortened version was given in this book's introduction). The following quote also speaks to this point. "So faith by itself, if it has no works, is dead" [James 2:17]. We can contrast the idea of acting with Paul's insistence that faith was all that was needed. In fact, Paul was against any action by the people (see chapter 2).

The United Nations has at least taken a stab at acting (mostly in the form of talk so far) through its Millennium Project in 2005. It set eight developmental goals:

1. Eradicate extreme poverty and hunger
2. Achieve universal primary education
3. Promote gender equality and empower women
4. Reduce child mortality
5. Improve maternal health
6. Combat HIV/AIDS, malaria, and other diseases
7. Ensure environmental sustainability
8. Develop a global partnership for development.

There were a total of eighteen specific targets and a plan for action. I can only hope that these good intentions are not forgotten.[4]

Peace, justice, understanding, and cooperation are possible. Yeshua's dominion of justice could be here on earth if everyone followed the Unitarian Universalist principles and other, similar statements of conscience. The enormous inequality in wealth we face is clearly

....
4   More information can be found at http://www.unmillenniumproject.org/reports/index.htm

the outcome of some people and corporations taking a disproportion-ate amount of it. This inequality becomes even more striking when we expand our view to include the entire world. The discrepancy between first-world nations, especially the United States, and third-world coun-tries is shameful. In moving toward equality, we must include sustain-ability. We cannot keep on over-consuming the world's resources. A simpler, less materialistic society is needed. Yeshua led a simple life.

While ideally people would voluntarily give up some of their wealth to help low-income families, thus following the message of Yeshua, this does not seem to happen very often. Many are deaf to the true message of Yeshua. When taxation of the wealthy is suggested as a means to help the poor, this action is denounced as "socialism!" Perhaps Yeshua was not just a liberal but also an early socialist.[5] Fortunately, a few outstand-ing people do give generously of their wealth, serving as examples to the rest.

Yeshua's program of social reform, if implemented, could indeed bring about the dominion of justice and heaven on earth. Of course, it was impossible to implement this vision in more than a small way in Yeshua's place and time. The Romans and their dominance system were simply too strong and entrenched for a peaceful revolution to change it. Can we do it now?

Perhaps today we might finally begin the real process. But special interests must first be put aside for the greater common good. Conflicts based on ethnic or religious lines must be settled somehow (this is a huge problem, vastly easier said than done). The problem of food, wa-ter, and shelter shortages must be solved (doable). Health issues must be addressed (also doable). Proper attention to these basic needs might greatly reduce the fighting. Quite likely, if the issues of food, water, shelter, and health were resolved for "the most inconspicuous mem-bers" of humanity—a goal that is within reach—then peace and justice might begin to appear on the scene. In the words of Amos [5:24], we would then "let justice roll down like waters, and righteousness like an ever flowing stream." It would take a relatively small percentage of the gross national products of the developed nations to achieve these

----

5 If we can believe Luke in his work, Acts, Yeshua's followers were communists. "They would sell their possessions and goods and distribute the proceeds to all, as any had need" [Acts 2:45].

goals. Apparently, all that is lacking is the concern and the resolve. Fortunately, some individuals and organizations are selflessly making headway toward rectifying the situation.

EPILOGUE FOR THIS PART

The title of this Part, and of the book itself, is "Meet Yeshua." Have we met him? Yes, no, and perhaps. I don't think that we are any closer to knowing much about the life of Yeshua. Some readers may now have some new information about him. Chapter 8 does include an important interpretation of Yeshua's healings. Chapters 7 and 9 have more information on who he was not, but that does not help with who he was.

But while we may not have met him, we are likely much better acquainted with what Yeshua stood for. As we have seen, many of his sayings have relevance for the world today. We have met his ideas and his important actions. He advocated for justice and equality. He associated with the poor, the disadvantaged, and the outcast. He brought them acceptance and hope, curing the social ill of ostracism. So perhaps or even yes, we have met Yeshua in what may be the only way possible.

When I started this project, I was looking for the human Jesus whom I came to call Yeshua. I now realize that I did not "find Yeshua"— rather, I found his message, including what he did. So going back to the Buddhist saying about confusing the finger pointing to the moon for the moon, I could say that I have now glimpsed the moon instead of the finger. Now I need to try to find more of the moon by acting on Yeshua's principles and actions. I hope you will join me.

Chapter 7:
Birth

This last Part, which is called "But What About...?" seeks to answer some of the residual questions you may have about the christology and mythology surrounding Jesus. Most of us have heard so many stories about the birth, miracles, and death of Jesus that I want to examine them briefly and give them an interpretation that is compatible with my Unitarian Universalist understanding. I am now putting aside the discussion of Yeshua the man. I will therefore switch to using mostly "Jesus" for the person of Christian myth. This is a deliberate move to emphasize the difference between the two figures: Yeshua, the man and teacher, and Jesus, the lead character in Christian mythology (although Mary seems to be a close second and sometimes even in the lead). I will still use "Yeshua" when talking about the human person.

VIRGIN BIRTH?

I start with the only statement that is consistent with rational thought: Jesus was not born of a miraculous virgin birth. However, it is worthwhile to examine the mythological virgin birth tale. There were good reasons for its creation. The colorful story has been embellished over the centuries to its current point, where it has little to do with the bible and far more to do with the dollar. But so much of our culture is wrapped up in it that we should try to see what there is behind it all.

The gospels of Matthew and Luke give two almost completely different stories of Jesus' birth, while the other gospels do not even mention it: Mark was totally silent, and John gave only a metaphorical allusion. Paul, who was the earliest writer from whom we have surviving manuscripts, included only minor statements about Jesus' birth and never mentioned Mary or Joseph. Neither the inferred Q gospel, which was early, nor the gospel of Thomas mentions his birth.

There are many incompatibilities between the accounts in Matthew and Luke. They give different reasons for Joseph and Mary's being in Bethlehem. The King Herod tale is found only in Matthew. It comes as a surprise to many people that the shepherds-and-manger story found in Luke lacks "kings" or a star, while Matthew has the star and three "kings" visiting Jesus in a house, but no shepherds. Our popular crèche scene with "kings" and shepherds together in a stable beneath a star does not exist in the bible. (See the section on Matthew below to find why I put "kings" in quotes.)

The birth stories may have been added to the gospels of Matthew and Luke at a later time. Each of these gospels makes perfect sense if it starts with its respective chapters 3. We know that Matthew and Luke copied from Mark, so it would have been reasonable to start their accounts where Mark did—that is, with their chapters 3. Thus I hypothesize that the writers in fact did begin at this point. Perhaps, after they had finished the first versions of their gospels, they heard about a new birth tradition with Jesus as a descendant of David, born in Bethlehem, with Mary and Joseph and the virgin birth, and then created their own myths based on these few details. This guess does help resolve a lingering question about the independence of the two writers: if they were independent from each other, why were there some similarities in the two birth stories? Then again, the birth stories could have been added by later writers.

The writers of the two gospels most likely knew about all of the miraculous births in Greek and Roman mythology. However, they (especially Matthew) also wanted to link Jesus to passages in the Hebrew Testament, seeking to show that Jesus' life was prophesied there. Matthew and especially Luke appear to have been familiar with only the Greek translation of the Hebrew Testament. Their concept of a virgin birth may have come in part from a mistranslation of a Hebrew word that merely meant "young woman" into Greek as "virgin." Possibly, Matthew and Luke combined this mistranslation with Greek mythology involving gods mating with humans to build their stories. Early English translations from the Greek kept the word as "virgin." The NRSV version corrects the translation to read, "The young woman is with child and shall bear a son, and shall name him Immanuel" [Isaiah 7:14]. It does not say that a "virgin shall conceive," but that a young woman is pregnant. Further, the passage in Isaiah refers to an event for those immediate times, not a future messiah. The name "Immanuel, God with us" does not imply a person who is divine; it only signifies a promise of God's help. In the Hebrew Testament, the child was not even called Immanuel after all! In some early religions, people used to sacrifice virgins, but in Christianity, they created a virgin. (I am sorry that I do not know who first said this and thus cannot give proper credit.)

Paul did not cite a virgin birth, but "born of woman" [Gal 4:4]. Furthering his non-divine birth story, Paul also used the phrase "descended from David *according to the flesh* and was *declared* to be Son of God...by *resurrection from the dead*" [Rom 1:3-4, emphasis added]. Paul possibly came up with the idea of "descended from David" from the then common expectation that a warrior descendant of David would free the Jews from Rome (see chapter 1). Mathew and Luke might have seen or heard of Paul's idea.

It is not clear who the father of Jesus was. "Joseph" may have been a fabricated name. The passage in Mark [6:3, NRSV] that reads in part, "Is not this...the son of Mary?" is unusual, since the usage "son of a woman" often implied that the father was not known. Occasionally, this expression was used after the father had died. Several other gospel passages suggest that Mary might have been a single mother, at least later on, since she is mentioned without any reference to a husband, let alone Joseph. Some even suggest that Mary was raped by (or had an affair with) a Roman soldier. One story in early rabbinic writings mentions a Roman soldier named Panthera (or Ben Pandera or Ben Pantere) who had relations with a young Jewish woman [Meier vol 1 p 96; see also Tabor pp 64-72].

The gospel of John contains an implication of an extramarital birth for Jesus, since the crowd said to Jesus, "We are not illegitimate children" [John 8:41, NRSV]. Several scholars speculate that "Joseph" was recruited to wed Mary to save her from the stigma of a birth out of wedlock. It is quite reasonable to suppose that the gossip that Mary was pregnant before her marriage was still around in Matthew and Luke's time and helped spur the invention of a miraculous conception to cover up the otherwise embarrassing situation.

The birth stories try to show that Jesus had a legitimate claim to be the "King of the Jews," with Matthew and Luke adding the appropriate "genealogies." But the Davidic genealogy is very weak in both of these gospels, which do not agree on much of the family tree. Even so, they had to strain through some very fuzzy parts, involving minor women and illegitimate births. The lineage was traced back through Joseph. Of course, the whole idea of Jesus being a descendant of David through Joseph is totally contradicted by the assertion in Matthew and Luke that it was not Joseph but God who was the father. Some scholars think that the Davidic lineage concept originated after Jesus' death. The "son of David" idea may have come from people believing his healings and thinking back to Solomon, who was also an exorcist and healer. In the Hebrew Testament, Solomon was the actual son of David, so that is a possible link.

The gospel of Luke seems to contradict the full implications of the birth story in which Joseph and Mary were told that their son would be the special "Son of God." Luke stated in a later passage that Jesus' family did not understand what was happening in the fictional Temple scene at age twelve.[1] "'Why have you been looking for me?' he said to them. 'Didn't you know that I have to be in my Father's house?' But they did not understand what he was talking about" [Luke 2:49–50]. If they had had this wonderful declaration, wouldn't they have believed in all that he did and said?

Joseph is not mentioned again in Matthew after the birth story. Possibly, he died and Mary remarried. Luke makes another passing reference to Joseph: "Isn't this Joseph's son?" [Luke 4:22b]. The gospel of John mentions Joseph twice. Maybe Joseph never existed but was a creation of the writers. John Shelby Spong states flatly, "Joseph is from start to finish a mythological character, created out of whole cloth, by the author of the gospel we call Matthew" [Spong 2007 p 32; see elsewhere in that reference for more details]. That both Matthew and Luke mention Joseph indicates either that there was an existing fable that they both drew on (which goes against Spong's suggestion), or that Luke depended somehow on Matthew. The mention of Joseph by John probably came from that author having seen the work of at least one of the earlier writers.

----

1 As a further indication that the Temple story at age twelve is fictional, the next-but-one verse [Luke 2:52] is based on 1 Samuel 2:26; such repetition from the Hebrew Testament always suggests a likely fabrication.

NAZARETH, BETHLEHEM, OR ELSEWHERE?

The Bethlehem tradition perhaps came from researching the Hebrew Testament, where Matthew and Luke found, "But you, O Bethlehem of Ephrathah, who are one of the little clans of Judah, from you shall come forth for me one who is to rule in Israel, whose origin is from old, from ancient days" [Micah 5:2].

Jesus was very likely born in Nazareth. Other parts of the bible do not mention this town, nor did contemporary historians and mapmakers, which has led some people to suggest that the town of Nazareth did not even exist in the time of Jesus. However, archeological work at Nazareth indicates that an older village at the site was abandoned and then resettled in the second century BCE.

It has been suggested that the name of the birth town came from confusion over references to him as "the Nazorean."[2] This reference to him could have morphed to "the Nazarene," which would imply someone coming from the town of Nazareth.

Robert Price states there was an early sect called "the Nazoreans," their name meaning "the Keepers" of the Torah. They were possibly related to a group mentioned in Jeremiah [Jer 35:1–10] and may have been itinerant carpenters [Price p 53]. Observe that the reference to carpenters relates to the controversy about whether Yeshua was a carpenter, which was discussed in chapter 3. Price thinks that originally people called him "Jesus the Nazorean" and not "Jesus the Nazarene" [Price p 54].

The term Nazorean might instead refer to a branch of the Essenes, though the current thinking is that Yeshua was not a member of that group. In chapter 1 a reference to the "natzorim" posits it as a possible origin of the town name.

Matthew further complicates things in this passage: "[Joseph] was instructed in a dream to go to Galilee; so he went there and settled in a city called Nazareth. So the prophecy uttered by the prophets came true: 'He will be called a Nazorean'" [Matt 2:22b–23]. Note that Matthew juxtaposes the two names. Further, there is no such prediction in any part of the Hebrew Testament.

....
2 For example, in many places in Acts, the NRSV Bible states in footnotes that Jesus was called "the Nazorean" in the original Greek writing. "Nazorean" is also found in Matthew 26:71 and John 18:7, 19:19 (NRSV).

The author of the gospel of John did not appear to know anything about the Bethlehem story (or chose to ignore it). Here are two passages that show that he believed that Yeshua was from Nazareth, or at least Galilee (Bethlehem was in Judea).

> Philip finds Nathanael and tells him, "We've found the one Moses wrote about in the Law, and the prophets mention too: Jesus, Joseph's son, from Nazareth." "From Nazareth?" Nathanael said to him. "Can anything good come from that place?" [John 1:45–46a]
>
> When they heard this declaration, some in the crowd said, "This man has to be the Prophet." "The Anointed!" others said. Still others objected: "Is the Anointed to come from Galilee?" [John 7:40–41]

Then there is the stubborn story that Yeshua was born in a cave near Bethlehem. Constantine built the "Church of the Nativity" in about 340 CE at the location of a cave that local people insisted was Jesus' birthplace. There is some support for the cave theory. For example, Justin Martyr mentioned the cave in the second century CE [Jerome Murphy-O'Connor, *Bible Review*, Feb 2000]. Matthew clearly stated the birth was in a house. Luke was less clear, saying that Yeshua was put in a feeding trough since there was no room for them in the lodge, suggesting that it was near an inn and not in a cave outside of town.

Another hypothesis is that he was born in Capernaum, which he used as a base for much of his ministry. Yet another scholar has suggested that perhaps there was a town near Nazareth, also called Bethlehem, where Mary went because of the gossip in Nazareth that she was pregnant with another man's child [Chilton p 8].

So let's just go with "born in Nazareth."

MATTHEW'S STORY

I will stay with Mathew's story for a while. Matthew put Joseph and Mary in residence in Bethlehem to begin with. They were in a house and not a stable for the birth. Matthew loved to find sources for his gospel in the Hebrew Testament. The gifts of the Magi are likely to have been inspired by Isaiah.

Nations shall come to your light, and kings to the brightness of your dawn...They shall bring gold and frankincense, and shall proclaim the praise of the Lord. [Isa 60:3, 6b]

The mention of spices may have come from the following passage. "Then she gave the king one hundred twenty talents of gold, a great quantity of spices, and precious stones; never again did spices come in such quantity as that which the queen of Sheba gave to King Solomon" [1 Kings 10:10]. The gospel of Matthew does not use the expression "kings" for the visitors. Instead, they are called "wise men," Magi, or astrologers, depending on which translation you use. Matthew also did not specify the number of the Magi. So according to Matthew, there were neither "We Three Kings" nor shepherds. However, later traditions set the number as three, and by the fifth century they had been identified as kings and given names.

Other problems cloud the "wise men" story. A star cannot suddenly appear and stay in one spot. But at that time, the sky was understood by many to be a vault only a little way above earth with the motion controlled by the gods, so it was reasonable then to talk of a star appearing, guiding, and then stopping. Matthew may have been inspired by a passage in the Hebrew Testament: "A star shall come out of Jacob, and a scepter shall rise out of Israel" [Num 24:17b]. Many people have searched ancient records for something like a supernova or a comet to account for the star. Nothing fits.

Simo Parpola [*Bible Review*, December 2001] believes that possibly the "star" referred instead to an important astrological event. He found references in the Babylonian records for a rare appearance of Jupiter and Saturn, an event that modern calculations confirm: Jupiter and Saturn were close together in Pisces for eleven months. They both followed retrograde paths and had three conjunctions during that period. This phenomenon recurred only in 786 and 1583 CE. Because of the retrograde motion, both planets would appear to "stop" their motions with regard to the background stars, but at different times. Interestingly, this event happened in 7 BCE, which is the earliest commonly accepted date for the birth of Jesus.

There is no historical record of Herod ordering the killing of male babies. This story was invented by Matthew, who viewed Jesus as the second Moses. Thus it might have been a reference to the Pharaoh ordering the killing of male Hebrew babies (spurring Moses' caretaker to save him by setting him adrift in a small boat). Then again, it might have referred to the final plague in the Passover story, in which all the first-born sons were killed by God, except for those of the Israelites. Matthew probably used the flight of Joseph, Mary, and the infant Jesus to Egypt as a way to link still another Hebrew Testament passage to his story: "'Out of Egypt I have called my son'" [Matt 2:15b], and as a way to get the family to Galilee. Matthew appears to have based the Moses saga on the account given by Josephus, rather than the Hebrew Testament [Price p 63].

LUKE'S STORY

Luke had a much more elaborate story, starting with a birth story for John the Baptizer, who was allegedly a cousin of Jesus. Luke then switched to the birth of Jesus. Interestingly, Luke wrote almost as many verses about John as about Jesus in his birth story.

Luke mentioned some events that are inconsistent with each other and the historical record. One of them was, "In those days it so happened that a decree was issued by Emperor Augustus that a census be taken of the whole civilized world" [Luke 2:1]. Luke was referring to a census that actually did take place when Quirinius was governor of Syria. However, this census took place in 6 CE, which is not compatible with Luke's earlier phrase "In the days of Herod," as Herod died in 4 BCE. This historical census was only for Judea (not "the whole civilized world") and did not apply to Galilee. Further, no census ever required a person to return to an ancestral home. Instead, what was wanted was a count of who was living where at the time.

Luke wrote that Joseph and Mary lived in Nazareth and, following Luke's illogical premises, had to travel to Bethlehem for the census. Even if this were so, Mary would not have been required to go. Because of all the people who allegedly had to go to Bethlehem, there was "no room at the inn," giving us the stable scene with the shepherds, but no wise men—nor any star over the manger. Luke's heavenly messenger with the heavenly host may have symbolically represented the hope for the overthrow of the Roman rule. "A savior was born to you—he is the anointed...On earth peace to people whom he has favored" [Luke 2:11b, 14b]. Luke's story has clear references to various parts of the Hebrew Testament [see Price pp 58–59]. Unlike Matthew, Luke [2:22–39] held that there was no problem with going to Jerusalem, where Herod was, and remaining there for a few days—Herod was not a threat, in Luke's story.

Luke is the only gospel author to mention anything about the childhood of Jesus and then with only the one reference to a fictitious Temple visit [Luke 2:42–49]. The "Infant Gospel," in which Jesus was shown as impulsive and petulant, has been discredited.

Here is a question that has no answer. If Jesus had such a wondrous birth and had been declared the "Son of God," why did it take up to thirty years for him to start a ministry? Wouldn't he have used his divine powers and understanding to spread his message earlier, maybe as a teenager? After all, Luke noted that at age twelve, "Everyone listening to him was astounded at his understanding and responses" [Luke 2:47]. Luke probably drew on various traditions of Hebrew prophets doing something special at the age of twelve.

BIRTH DATE?

The birth stories in the gospels give no indication of the season or month, aside from Luke mentioning shepherds in the fields, suggesting a warm time of the year. This lack of a definite time of the year is odd, since many events in the bible were tied to the time of a festival. Some sources say that Hippolytus, writing in about 200 CE, was the first to refer to December 25 as Jesus' birth date. One popular explanation is that this was the date of the birth/rebirth of Mithras, the sun god in Zoroastrianism,[3] who was very popular in Roman times, especially among the soldiers who had traveled to Persia. The date of course is linked to the winter solstice. See Robert Price [pp 43–46] for a more complete discussion of this point.

However, some scholars favor another theory on the origin of the December 25 birth date. The main objection to this date deriving from pagan origins is that the early Christians adopted December 25 at a time when they were trying very hard to separate themselves from the Roman pagans who were all around them. Only much later did the Catholics begin purposely adopting pagan dates. Pagan customs like a

3 Rodney Stark takes exception, saying that Mithras was a new god and not the same as the Persian sun god Mitra [Stark 2007 p 140].

tree or mistletoe were co-opted perhaps starting in the twelfth century. So how did December 25 get established? To the early church the birth was of little importance, compared to Easter. One theory says that because March 25 was thought to be the date of the crucifixion of Jesus, early Christians decided that he must have been conceived on that date as well, making a closed circle in time. Nine months later, it was December 25.[4]

One theory is as good as another. There really is nothing upon which to base a birth date. However, in spite of all of this, the two stories of the birth do offer a rich set of images that can be read as metaphors for the birth of a new hope and a new message. I and other Unitarian Universalists do enjoy the season, feeling quite comfortable with the rich pagan elements and rites.

OTHER SPECIAL BIRTHS

Why did Matthew and Luke need such birth stories? In the legends and stories of those times, no hero or important person had an ordinary birth, and in view of Jesus' peasant origins, the gospel authors had to make his very special. Matthew and Luke certainly did not invent the idea of a "son of god"; many other traditions allege divine births. Plato was said to have been Apollo's son. Other offspring of the gods include Alexander the Great, Pythagoras, Apollonius, and the heroes of myth: Perseus, Horus, and Hercules, to name a few. Special births were also attributed to the Roman emperors. This list is by no means complete. It would take us too far afield to delve into them here. Suffice it to note that virgin births were part of the Greco-Roman mythology of the times. The discussion by Charles Talbert, "Miraculous Conceptions and Births in Mediterranean Antiquity," elaborates on this theme [Levine et al. eds ch 4].

It is interesting to compare the biblical stories to the account of the birth of the Buddha in Paul Carus' book. Paraphrasing, we find that angels proclaimed a mighty son, an aged woman blessed the baby, and

---

4 An alternative date has been proposed for his birth: January 6 was used in Egypt and Asia Minor as the birth date; this date still is used by the Armenian Church. The January 6 date is based on an alternative timing of the crucifixion as being on April 6. But of course the crucifixion date is not known even though John Meier gives the date as "Friday, April 7, 30 CE" [Meier, vol. 1, p 406].

light flooded the world. Miracles occurred: the blind seeing, the deaf hearing and speaking, the lame walking, the crooked becoming straight, prisoners being freed, and streams becoming clear. Kings paid their respects. He was to bring deliverance to the world and rescue the poor [Carus pp 8–10].

So many things mentioned in this account resemble biblical stories that it is possible that some elements went one way or the other. The written story of the Buddha, although he was born about five centuries before Jesus, came several centuries after the Buddha's life. The source Carus referred to might have been written even later. The miracles of the blind, deaf, and lame, the aged woman (similar to Luke 2:36–38), the "crooked straight" (compare to Isaiah), the kings (Matthew), and the prophecies all have parallels in the bible. But this does not prove which way the stories traveled. Moreover, both could be leaning on still earlier traditions. In actuality, the birth and life of the person who became known as the Buddha are documented, but it is difficult to separate fact from later myth when it comes to his life. Karen Armstrong's book on the Buddha offers a more complete discussion of this point [Armstrong 2001, Introduction and ch 1]. His name was Siddhartha Gotama (also transliterated as Gautama). His father was an important person, a raja in some versions of the story, in a town called Kapilavatthu in northeast India, near or possibly inside what is now Nepal. He had an ordinary birth to a mortal woman sometime around the year 563 BCE.

Chapter 8:
Miracles

Jesus' miracles fall into two main categories: healing[1] stories and the control of nature. These can be called miracles or magic. The difference, according to John Dominic Crossan, lies in who is talking: if it is one's religion, then it is a miracle; otherwise, it is magic [Crossan 1991 p 305]. Marcus Borg likes to call the reported events "mighty deeds" or "deeds of power," rather than miracles. Otherwise, we can call them myths with messages.

SIGNS

The miracles are of course controversial. Possibly the purpose of the miracle stories was to serve as inducements to gain new followers. Some scholars think that all of the miracles were added by later writers, rather than coming from stories originating during Jesus' lifetime. The first layer of Q contains no miracles. The gospel writers appear to have created many of the miracle stories based on ones found in the Hebrew Testament. The earliest extant writings are the letters of Paul, who mentions no miracles, either his own or those of Jesus. One of Paul's letters [1 Cor 1:18–25] contains the phrase "For Jews demand signs,"[2] with the implication that Paul's gentile Christians did not.

A similar statement about signs is found in Mark 8:12:

> [Jesus] groaned under his breath and says, "Why does this generation insist on a sign? I swear to God, no sign will be given this generation!"

---

1 Except where it makes a difference, I am including exorcisms under the term "healings."

2 The usage of the word "signs" in the Bible usually means miracles.

118 »   BUT WHAT ABOUT

The phrase "no sign" would have meant that no miracle would be performed. However, Mark did include many "signs" in other places. The Jesus Seminar did not consider this passage authentic. The Christian Testament, especially in Acts, refers many times to "signs and wonders" being performed by Jesus' followers to convince people to convert. There was a general expectation that any great prophet would perform miracles, so the story of Jesus needed to include some. Mark might have added the miracle stories to fill that need. On the other hand, as noted in chapter 2, Josephus said that Jesus "was one who wrought surprising feats."

The Q gospel, in the Q^2 layer, does report some miracles. Mark had two sets of five miracles with some parallelism, but only the feeding of the multitude is repeated. Matthew also had ten miracle stories, reminiscent of the ten miracles/signs of Moses in Exodus. Matthew frequently used the expression "to fulfill what the prophets had said" about the miracles of Jesus, as well as for other activities. John incorporated seven "signs" in his gospel, making use of the special number seven. Some authorities think that John may have drawn on a "signs gospel." One attempted reconstruction of the "signs gospel" appears in *The Complete Gospels* [Miller ed pp 175–193].

The gospel writers, especially Matthew, wanted to tie Jesus to the prophets of the Hebrew Testament in order to show that he was the rightful heir to that line. Since Moses, Elijah, and Elisha all performed various physical miracles and healings, it was necessary to create stories showing Jesus accomplishing similar feats (see the Exodus story in the bible for Moses' miracles). Elijah multiplied a food supply, raised a person from the dead, and went straight to heaven [1 Kings 17:8–24]. Elisha cured a leper, multiplied food, and raised the dead [2 Kings 4:1–37]. Elijah and Elisha probably lived around 880 to 840 BCE and were from the northern part of Palestine, as Jesus later was.

There are other parallels in the Jewish literature. Honi the Circle Drawer could cause rain to start and stop. He got his nickname from drawing a circle on the ground and standing in it, petitioning God until the desired outcome was achieved. Hanina ben Dosa, who may have lived around the time of Yeshua, was another miracle worker. One story involves the curing of Rabbi Gamaliel's sick son at a distance. The details are not important here; what is significant is the close parallel of that cure at a distance to one in the gospels concerning a Roman officer's son (or servant) [Matt. 8:5–13 || Luke 7:1–10 || John 4:46–54].

Hanina ben Dosa was also noted for natural miracles. Honi and Hanina ben Dosa were not considered to work the miracles directly. Rather, they were said to have special abilities in asking favors of God. John Meier provides a detailed discussion of other healers [Meier vol 2 pp 576–588]. Geza Vermes also offers an insightful discussion of healers [Vermes 2000 pp 252–263], as does E. P. Sanders in his discussion of miracles [Sanders pp 132–168], which also includes nature miracles.

Healings are not found only in the Judeo-Christian church. Many other people were healers before, during, and after Jesus. There are many stories of healings that took place at Epidaurus in ancient Greece and Pergamum in Turkey at shrines to Asklepios (also transliterated as Asclepius), who was said to be the son of the god Apollo. Some of these healings are similar to those reported to have occurred at modern Catholic shrines. A Greek named Apollonius of Tyana, known as a healer and exorcist, was said to have raised the dead. (See Wendy Cotter, "Miracle Stories: the God Asclepius, the Pythagorean Philosophers, and the Roman Rulers" [Levine et al. eds ch 9].)

I believe that the evidence shows a *tradition* that "miracles" were worked by Jesus. Because Jesus possibly had a *reputation* as a healer earned during his lifetime, a discussion of his "miracles" is in order.

HEALINGS

An initial observation is that the healing stories may not have been meant as actual happenings. For instance, the "curing of the blind" could be a metaphor: people at first were "blind" to the message of Yeshua but then "saw" it. Similarly, people were initially "deaf" to his message but then "heard" it. However, it is also reasonable to think that something more actually occurred.

Most (if not all) illnesses at that time were thought to be caused by either sins or demonic possession. It is not necessary to distinguish what kinds of ailments were being healed for our purposes here. Exorcisms, which appear much more commonly in the gospels than in the Hebrew Testament, represent the majority of the cures in the synoptic gospels, especially Mark. The gospel of John does not mention any exorcisms, possibly because author felt they sounded too much like magic. According to Geza Vermes, at that time "healing," "expelling demons," and "forgiving sins" were used rather interchangeably

[Vermes 2003 p 10]. The passage about a house divided against itself rather clearly shows that exorcisms were common, at least in the time of the gospel writers. The last sentence, aimed at Yeshua's accusers, shows that they also used exorcists:

> Every government against itself is devastated, and a house divided against a house falls. If Satan is divided against himself—since you claim I drive out demons in Beelzebul's name—how will his domain endure? If I drive out demons in Beelzebul's name, in whose name do your own people drive them out? [Luke 11:17–19a]

Mark portrayed Jesus more as a healer than a teacher. Everywhere he went, according to Mark, many people clamored to be cured. Many of Mark's healing stories involve "casting out demons." Robert Price says about the healings that "the strongest argument in favor of Jesus actually having been a faith healer is that virtually all the ailments he is said to have cured have a place on the list of psychogenic maladies or somatization disorders in today's diagnostic manuals" [Price p 151]. His book presents this case in more detail. The authors of the gospels, especially Mark, quite likely exaggerated the number of cures.

Some details of healings as reported in the gospels are at variance with the situation in the time of Yeshua, indicating creative writing. For example, in Mark, a paralytic is lowered through the roof after the tiles were removed; however, houses in the villages of that time did not have tiled roofs. Other clues point to the fabrication of details; for example, Mark 7:34 has Jesus using the expression "ephphatha" in curing a deaf person, which may come from Isaiah 35:5. Mostly Jesus healed only with words, and according to the gospels he never used amulets or potions.[3] However, Mark's use of the Aramaic words "ephphatha" (and also "talitha koum") in a Greek text probably sounded like magic spells to listeners. Jesus is reported to have said things like "your faith has cured you" or "your sins are forgiven." (Note carefully that the biblical wording used the passive voice, rather than the active "I forgive your sins." This distinction has a bearing on issues during his "trial" discussed in chapter 9.)

Many people were called healers and/or exorcists then. They were just humans; the title did not mean that they were special envoys of God. The Hebrew Testament never held that a messiah ("anointed person")

---

3 However, Jesus is reported to have used spit and mud to cure blindness.

would necessarily be a miracle worker or that a miracle worker was divine.

Did Yeshua really cure? We first need to distinguish between healing and curing. Curing means eliminating the disease or illness; it is about the body. Healing means to make one whole; it is about the mind and spirit. In some cases, healing means to accept and live with an illness that cannot be cured. One can always be healed, if not cured. (I speak as one who is living with cancer.) Sometimes the act of healing helps in the curing. I firmly believe in the healing powers of creativity and art. Even just experiencing something beautiful—a flower, a sunset, a beautiful piece of music, or just a moment of quiet reflection—can uplift my spirit. When the spirit soars, the body responds.

Bernie Siegel, in his book *Peace, Love, and Healing*, discusses the body-mind connection in healing. He points out that much healing falls outside of "conventional" medicine. I highly recommend this book for anyone interested in healing. Two of Siegel's stories illustrate this aptly. The first is about a young man who became a lawyer to please his parents rather than pursue a career as a violinist. But when he developed a brain tumor and was told that he had only one year to live, he decided to take up the violin for that year. By the end of the year, his tumor was gone and he had a job in an orchestra [Siegel p 183].

The other story [pp 9–10] concerns a 78-year-old landscape gardener who developed stomach cancer. Rather than having surgery immediately, he said that he needed to do some planting to make the world more beautiful and had his surgery a few weeks later. The subsequent report showed that the cancer had spread and thus not all was removed. The doctor suggested chemotherapy, but the gardener said he didn't have time for it; there was still planting to be done. Four years later, there was no sign of his cancer.

Bill Moyers made a public television series called *Healing and the Mind* and published a book, created largely from this PBS series, which includes many interviews with various people. This book contains the following observations. Ron Anderson opines, "In my view, mind/body medicine is really the art of medicine. We've done very well with the science of medicine…But we've set aside the art of medicine" [Moyers p 28]. Anderson later states that "many patients don't need a prescription, they need you to talk to them…What's wrong with that if it's healing?… But until we deal with the illness and the wholeness of that individual,

we are not good doctors" [pp 31, 37]. David Smith notes, "Most disease processes that we see get worse if we don't allow the mind to be
part of the healing process" [p 50]. John Zawacki says, "For example,
when physicians affirm people, they start to create a healing process...
Listening to people, and empowering them, and giving them a sense of
worth is directly related to healing" [pp 152, 154]. Rachel Naomi Remen
notes, "The reality is that healing happens between people" [p 319].
Later she says, "I think that's what healing is—evoking the will to live.
And it is evoked not by doing something, but by receiving another person, by letting another person know that their pain and their suffering
and their fear matters" [p 356]. The book also explores meditation, the
role of stress, and Chinese medicine.

Similarly, the book by Norman Cousins, *Head First: The Biology of
Hope and the Healing Power of the Human Spirit* shows the mind's power to affect the body and bring about a cure. Cousins also used humor
as a way of healing or even curing.

There is a renewed interest in the placebo effect. People given dum-
my pills in tests comparing a new medicine to a placebo often show
improvement, sometimes as great as from the drug being tested. Recent
experiments using brain scans show that placebos have a definite bio-
logical effect. Some medical scientists suggest that people's belief that
they are being helped actually produces a positive effect, though possibly this is instead due to the doctors' taking time to interact with the
patient. More research needs to be done, but these results tie into the
statements given in *Healing and the Mind* and to the healings of Jesus.

The above assertions, along with many others, clearly constitute a
sound basis for saying that the *healings* of Jesus could have been factual, at least in part. Keep in mind that healing is not the same as curing,
though healing can bring a cure in some cases. I have only scratched
the surface of the mind's power to heal; to do more here would take us
too far afield. Readers interested in more information on the mind-body
connection should check out *The Power of the Mind to Heal* by Joan
and Miroslav Borysenko and *The Cure Within. A History of Mind-Body
Medicine* by Anne Harrington.

The issue of healing can separate people of faith from those who
believe in a rational world of cause and effect—the world of modern
science. The healing stories are important to Christianity: they show the
divinity of Jesus, which is a simple explanation for them. However, this

is a circular argument: Jesus could heal because he was divine, and the healing proves his divinity.

It is difficult to explain all healings in modern medical terms. There are cures and remissions that doctors cannot explain. But an unexplained cure does not mean a divine intervention. Even today, claims of healing miracles abound, for example at various shrines where healings are said to occur. But although many crutches have been left at the various shrines, they have few if any dark glasses, no artificial limbs, and certainly no coffins.

A good documentation of mental illness during the Algerian revolt against France appears in the book *The Wretched of the Earth,* by the psychiatrist Frantz Fanon. Many parallels exist between the illnesses reported in that book and those in the gospels. I refer interested readers to the discussion found in John Dominic Crossan [Crossan 1991 pp 317–318]. Obery Hendricks Jr. refers to the same book [Hendricks pp 53–54].

Many alternative forms of healing are around today. Acupuncture, qigong, and Reiki and other energy healings produce a positive outcome at least some of the time.

Here is the crux of Yeshua's healings, as I see it. *He brought humanity back to these marginalized people by openly accepting them. He touched them both literally and figuratively.* Specifically, the ills caused by ostracism were healed by acceptance.

Wayne-Daniel Berard states that only a person who has been marginalized him/herself knows the right words to say to make someone feel worthwhile and no longer an outsider [Berard p 76]. This worthless feeling was indeed a demon that needed to be exorcised. Jesus was quoted many times as having said words to this effect: "Your sins are forgiven." To get closer to what Yeshua might have meant, this can easily be reinterpreted as something like, "Whatever you did doesn't matter. You are now a welcomed member of society." Jesus elsewhere said things like "your trust (or faith) has made you well." This phrase too can be interpreted along similar lines: "By believing in the redeeming power of acceptance, you have made yourself well," which also might be closer to the spirit of Yeshua.

A similar acceptance of outcasts is found in Buddhism. The Buddha accepted all people regardless of their status or caste, simply because they were people. The rejects of society found understanding and acceptance, perhaps for the first time, and regained their self-respect

[Smith p 89]. I am not trying to suggest that Yeshua was influenced by the Buddha but rather to show the universal power of acceptance.

The tale of the "Demon of Gerasa" [Mark 5:1-13], while filled with inconsistencies, does offer a clue. Jesus asked the demon what its name was, and the reply was "My name is Legion." This was very likely a reference to the "illness" of having many Roman Legions (a unit of troops) in Palestine (for although there were not many troops in Galilee at that time, there were many nearby)—or perhaps, more generally, to the Roman rule by military power.

I think that we can dismiss the stories of raising the dead. During the time of Jesus, people were not declared dead until three days had elapsed (this number will crop up again in discussion of the crucifixion in chapter 9), probably because whereas there was no easy way at that time to detect signs of life when someone was unconscious or in a coma, experience showed that some people would in fact regain consciousness. The story of raising a widow's dead son [Luke 7:11-17] likely comes from the similar story of Elijah [1 Kings 17:17-24; also see Weyler pp 197-198]. Again, similarities to the Hebrew Testament raise the flag of possible fanciful writing.

NATURE MIRACLES

The feeding of the multitudes (the miracle of the loaves and fish) appears many times in the gospels, even twice in Mark and Matthew [Mark 6:35-44 and again in 8:1-9 with a reprisal in Mark 8:14-21 || Matt 14:15-21 and repeated in 15:32-38 || Luke 9:12-17 || John 6:1-15]. In Mark, the disciples do not believe that this could happen, even the second time around. The size of the crowd varies from story to story, but it is always in the thousands, which is almost for certain a gross exaggeration, given the low population density in rural Galilee back then. The Hebrew Testament's stories of Elijah and Elisha's multiplying food, cited above, may lie behind this story. Those cases concerned food for only a few people, but the gospel writers needed to make the story better.

Numerology appears to be a strong theme in these stories. In one case, there are five loaves and two fish for a total of the mystical number seven. Another version has seven loaves. The baskets of food left over total twelve, also a special number.

In John, the feeding occurs on Passover for people who could not get to Jerusalem, with that added symbolism. All of this is rather simply explained by Yeshua's message of sharing: when everyone shares, there is enough to go around—as in the well-known story of Stone Soup, in which people bring what little they have to make soup for everyone.

The changing of water to wine in the gospel of John [2:1–10] probably was inspired by the cult of Dionysus at Eleia, where such a transformation was presented as part of an annual festival. The author of John was likely Greek and well aware of this legend.

Stilling a storm has roots in the story of Jonah but also may have come from Psalm 107:25, 29–30 and Nahum 1:4a. In addition, Pythagoras was also reported to have calmed the seas.

Walking on water must simply be dismissed, although some authors try to explain it away by saying that Jesus was on a nearby shore or in very shallow water. There is a story of a preacher who told his congregation that if they had enough faith, he could walk on water. When they responded that they believed, the preacher replied, "If you believe it, then I don't need to do it! And if you don't believe, then I am not able."

Thich Nhat Hanh has a nice take on miracles. He said, "To live in the present moment is a miracle. The miracle is not to walk on water. The miracle is to walk on the green earth in the present moment, to appreciate the peace and beauty that are available now" [Hanh p 1].

It is noteworthy that only a very few people, usually just the disciples, witnessed most of the nature miracles (excepting the feeding of the multitudes). It is almost as if the miracles were "secrets." This fact makes it even more likely that these events were figments of the authors' imaginations. In any event, reports of the nature miracles seem to have had little effect in making people believe and become followers.

The story of Jesus cursing a fig tree [Mark 11:12–14 and 11:20–21 || Matt 21:18–20] because it had no fruit, even though it was not the season for it, is difficult to explain even in metaphorical terms, since it is so out of character for the Yeshua that we have met. Some scholars say that this story refers to the destruction of the Temple, which probably occurred just before Mark wrote his gospel and thus had nothing to do with Jesus.

   Some of the miracles can be characterized as propaganda implying that "things go better with Jesus." When Jesus was present the seas were calmer, the journey shorter, the food more plentiful, the fish catch bigger, and so on.

Chapter 9:
Death and Beyond

INTRODUCTION

Jesus' last week, crucifixion, and resurrection are central to Christianity. This is an interesting subject for Unitarian Universalists to examine, since we do not believe in a divine Christ figure. How might a non-trinitarian view these events? Are there any facts behind the mythology? This chapter briefly covers Jesus' death and what happened afterward. Innumerable books have been written on just this subject. The importance of the last week is reflected in the Christian Testament, where the gospels devote between 22 percent (Luke) and 44 percent (John) of their length[1] to that final week. So it is fitting that we take some time to look at this topic to see how the various stories might have originated. There are no final answers to the questions surrounding Jesus' last week. I am presenting only possible interpretations.

Most likely Yeshua knew that his calling for a change to the social structure would be unacceptable to the priestly class and the Roman authorities. He must have known that his mission was a risky endeavor that could possibly lead to his death. He had a clear warning in the execution of John the Baptizer, who was put to death for saying that a major change would soon take place (see chapter 3). The gospels state that Jesus predicted his coming death and resurrection. I personally believe that Yeshua likely thought, and may have even stated, that he might be executed when he went to Jerusalem on what became his last trip. He may even have wanted it, believing that his martyrdom would

----

1   The percentages are approximate, as they are based on a quick page count of the gospels as found in the NRSV bible.

help his cause. This hypothesis explains why passages in the gospels refer to him predicting his own death.

In what may be the earliest writings (the first level of the Q), there is no mention of Yeshua's life or death: the focus is on his teachings. The letters of Paul give no details of Yeshua's death but state only that he was crucified. We cannot rely on any of the details about the last week as given in the gospels, since they differ among the four renditions. Of course, the authenticity of these parts of the gospels is suspect, for they were written after the Easter myth had been created.

PALM SUNDAY

The accounts of Palm Sunday in the gospels are likely the creation of Mark [11:1–11], copied by Matthew and Luke. If anything like the reported entry into Jerusalem had taken place, especially the versions in Matthew and Luke, not only Jesus but his followers as well would have faced immediate arrest and execution. In several well-documented instances, similar groups approaching Jerusalem were savagely attacked and killed by the Romans, who would have reacted immediately to anyone being called a king or the son of David. The passage in Mark, "Blessed is the one who comes in the name of the Lord! Blessed is the coming kingdom of our father David" [11:9–10], does not explicitly call Jesus either king or the son of David, but the "coming kingdom of David" would have been a red flag. Matthew [21:9] called Jesus the "son of David," while Luke [19:38] and John [John 12:15] used "king."

Casting further doubt on the actuality of this event is the fact that much of the wording was taken from the Hebrew Testament—always an indication of possible inauthenticity. Jesus' riding into Jerusalem on a colt was based on Zechariah 9:9. Matthew flubbed his version of the entry into the city; he has Jesus riding on both a donkey *and* a colt [Matt 21:4–6]. The shouts of "Blessed is the one who comes in the name of the Lord!" came from Psalm 118:26.

E. P. Sanders makes an interesting observation. A person could not partake in the Passover celebration without first being purified in Jerusalem of any uncleanliness. Most pilgrims would have become unclean through various acts of everyday life. The purification process took one week, so they needed to arrive in Jerusalem at least a week before Passover. As a devout Jew, Jesus would have arrived no later than on Thursday. Thus "Palm Sunday" may have been before Sunday [Sanders p 250].

It is uncertain whether this was Jesus' only trip to Jerusalem for Passover. Since all Jews were supposed to go to Jerusalem for all the major festivals, it seems probable that Jesus had made other trips there in spite of the long distance. Luke implies that other trips took place in his youth,[2] and John explicitly lists three trips during Jesus' ministry. If this final trip was his only one, then why did he go there this time? I have no answer to this question.

TEMPLE SCENE

The synoptic gospels state that the "cleansing of the Temple" took place during Jesus' final week. In the gospel of John, however, this event occurs two years earlier, without any negative consequences at the time. (Recall the discussion of this act in chapter 4.) It is doubtful that anything more than a very minor confrontation occurred, if anything at all, since any larger disturbance would have resulted in an immediate arrest. The Romans were on special alert to quash any disturbances during the holy festivals, when huge crowds of pilgrims meant things could quickly get out of hand.[3]

Since many scholars link the Temple disturbance to Jesus' death, I will discuss this scene as if it did occur during his final week. Several scholars think that the "cleansing" scene was one of the few acts of Jesus that actually happened [see Funk 1998 pp 121–122, for example]. The synoptics say that Jesus went several times to preach in the Temple *after* the "cleansing" scene without being arrested. His preaching allegedly attracted large crowds and was critical of the priesthood. Since the priests and Romans allowed this to happen (again, assuming this account has any merit), he is not likely to have been marked as a troublemaker. According to the synoptics, he was not arrested during these visits because the priests feared the crowd would turn ugly.

2   "Now his parents used to go to Jerusalem every year for the Passover festival. And when he was twelve years old, they went up for the festival as usual" [Luke 2:41–42].

3   This is the reason that Pilate was in Jerusalem so that he could react immediately to any disturbance. Normally, he was in Caesarea.

Of course, the entire "cleansing" story might not have been literally true but rather meant as a metaphor against Temple practices, with
Jesus' subsequent visits being merely an excuse to introduce more sayings and teachings. It is a risky bet that there is any truth to the Temple
story.

THE "LAST SUPPER" AND BETRAYAL

Passover was a single day, followed by a week of unleavened bread.
Accounts of the "Last Supper" are problematic, those in the synoptics
being at odds with that found in John. The synoptics all have this final
meal as a Passover meal and include a bread-and-wine offering. The
gospel of John, on the other hand, puts the final meal a day earlier; it
thus is not a Passover meal [John 13:1–12], and there is no bread-and-
wine ceremony. Instead, Jesus washes the feet of his disciples. The day
of the week of the final meal is crucial to the following "arrest and trial"
events. John Meier, in his very thorough manner, spends eighteen pages
on this issue, not counting footnotes. When it comes to the time of the
final meal, he sides with the day as given in John, that is, the day before
Passover [Meier vol 1 pp 383–400].

There are problems with the bread-and-wine part of the "Last
Supper" as it appears in the synoptics. It is very contrary to Judaism.
The very idea of "drinking blood" would have been totally repulsive to
Jews, even as a metaphor. Any contact with blood rendered a person
unclean, and drinking blood is explicitly prohibited in the Torah [Lev
17:10]. The idea of eating someone's body, even symbolically, would
have been similarly repellent.

The first written account, chronologically speaking, of the bread-
and-wine ceremony with the blood and body allusions (later called the
eucharist[4]) is found in the letters of Paul. Paul was writing for a largely gentile audience that would not have shared the Jews' revulsion to
blood. Paul gave this account of the ceremony:

> For I received from the Lord what I also handed on to you, that
> the Lord Jesus on the night when he was betrayed took a loaf
> of bread, and when he had given thanks, he broke it and said,
> "This is my body that is for you. Do this in remembrance of

---

4 From the Greek word for "we give thanks."

me." In the same way he took the cup also, after supper, saying, "This cup is the new covenant in my blood. Do this, as often as you drink it, in remembrance of me." [1 Cor 11:23–25]

In contrast, neither Mark's nor Matthew's account uses the expression "do this in remembrance of me" or asks that it become a repeated ritual. In John, the piece of bread is for the "betrayer"—it definitely is not part of a "blood-and-body" ceremony. In the passage above, Paul did not explicitly link the time of this ceremony to Passover, but only to the time of the "betrayal." Paul might have created the eucharist story to connect his new church to the Greek mystery cults, where such practices did occur. Some suggest that Paul also called on practices from Persian religion. Some of the Easter story is possibly based on legends of Tammuz, a god-man from the old religion of Canaan [Weyler pp 166–167, 171]. Observe that Paul was once more claiming to rely on a direct word "from on high." Exactly how the bread-and-wine tradition entered the synoptics remains unknown, but it likely derived from Paul's influence.

The Didache, as mentioned in chapter 2, is one of the very earliest relevant documents, perhaps rooted in a time prior to Paul's writing. In its earliest layer (Section 10), the eucharist is a pure thanksgiving for food and drink [Milavec p 25]. A later layer (Section 9) explicitly mentions wine and bread, but "blood-and-body" allusions are absent [Milavec p 23]. So these associations apparently were not part of the earliest traditions. Also, in Section 9 of the Didache the order is first wine then bread—just the opposite of the order in Paul.

In short, I think that the "Last Supper" is a myth created to fit in with the developing Christ story, possibly to link the new movement back to the Exodus story and Passover. I refer interested readers to Burton Mack, who gives more reasons to think thusly [Mack 1995 pp 87–91].

It is not clear that there was a betrayal, even though Paul mentions it in the quotation above. Again, it is suspicious that some of the text of the betrayal accords with wording in the Hebrew Testament. Some scholars think that Judas was a fictional character added after the Jesus movement split from Judaism and the "blame the Jews" sickness had begun. For one thing, "Judas" or "Jude" can refer to all of the people of Judea. Paul clearly refers to "the Twelve," not the eleven, at a time *after* Jesus' death. If the gospel stories of Judas are correct, only eleven disciples should be left. The "gospel of Judas," which made a big splash not too long ago, has since been reevaluated. Its first translation is now thought to have been incorrect in several places. Judas was condemned in it after all. But this whole gospel probably has no historical validity.

ARREST AND TRIAL

After the "Last Supper," the synoptics report that Jesus went to Gethsemane (Mark and Matthew) or the Mount of Olives (Luke). The scene in Luke may have been inspired by a passage concerning David [2 Sam 15:30–31]. Jesus' words, wherever they were spoken, are reported in the gospels, yet there is no way that anyone could have known them, since Jesus is said to have been by himself at the time. Nevertheless he is quoted as saying, "Father, if you choose, take this cup away from me!" [Luke 22:42a]. This passage may have been based on the death of Socrates, who drank a cup of poison—an allusion that would have been familiar to Greek speakers.

Immediately following this passage is the arrest scene, with "Judas" leading the arresting authorities (the gospels differ on who they were). Why was Judas needed in the story? Yeshua appears to have been well-known to the priests, so no identifier would have been needed. One speculation is that Jesus had a twin (see the End Note of chapter 3), and someone was needed to tell who was who.

So who arrested Jesus, where, and why? The answer remains murky. The high priests, noting that Jesus had a large following and preached against the status quo, may have feared that the Romans might begin a massive arrest-and-slaughter campaign, as they had done on previous occasions. There is a passage in John to this point:

> If we let [Jesus] go on like this, everybody will come to believe in him. Then the Romans will come and destroy our holy place and our nation...Don't you realize that it's to your advantage to have one person die for the people and not have the whole nation wiped out? [John 11:48, 50]

The problem with the "Temple scene" being the reason for the arrest is discussed in the previous section and in chapter 4. Some writers suggest that Yeshua was arrested because of his "political" activities. Perhaps his preaching about the "Kingdom of God" appeared to the Romans to be a political revolution. The priests may have told the Romans about Yeshua's calling for a needed change, twisting it into a political activity rather than just a social reform. I think it likely that the priests had Jesus arrested quietly at some time and place that will never be known, and turned him over to the Romans. If the Romans had arrested Yeshua, it is unlikely that any of his followers would have escaped as the gospels report them to have done. The Romans took no chances.

The trial scene is entirely fictional. We can read in the gospels that none of Jesus' followers witnessed it. Where could the information have come from, including who said what? There are many other reasons to view this event as a work of creative writing. As many writers point out, a "trial" was totally contrary to the Torah and Jewish practices. First, according to the synoptics, the arrest and questioning were at night, on Passover, with the questioning in the home of the High Priest—all conditions that would have been in violation of the Law. True, the gospel of John has all of this occurring the night before Passover, which removes one of the objections. But even so, no trial could happen at night or in a home. Jewish law required two independent witnesses to agree. But in Mark [14:56], we find that "although many gave false evidence against him, their stories didn't agree."[5]

Continuing with the problems of the trial, we note that what Jesus allegedly said was not considered blasphemy. Saying "your sins are forgiven" certainly was not, since the passive voice implies the forgiveness as being by someone else, possibly God. Claiming to be a messiah was not blasphemy because it did not connote divinity, nor did quoting Daniel on "one like the son of man." All Jews were considered the children of God. Wayne-Daniel Berard offers a more complete discussion of the foregoing problems [p 199–203]. Geza Vermes agrees that almost every portion of the account of the trial is in conflict with all aspects of Jewish law and practices [Vermes 2000 p 181].

Further, the different gospels report a diversity of locations of the "trial": before the High Council, before Pilate, before Herod Antipas, in various combinations thereof, and with different words said. If his execution were for religious reasons, as the gospels imply, he would not have been crucified by the Romans but stoned by the Jews in accord with the usual Jewish sentence for religious infractions.

5 Matthew [26:60b–61] did state that finally two witnesses did agree, but about a very minor point, certainly not anything blasphemous.

Probably the priests advised Pilate that Jesus was a troublemaker, and that ended the story. Jesus was probably condemned to death without any trial. The Romans were not known to have had much of a justice system for people who were not Roman citizens. A Roman crucifixion implied a political crime, such as treason or leading a rebellion. In this case, it would have been highly unusual for the Romans not to have arrested and executed at least some of his followers as well. However, we do have the example of John the Baptizer, where only the leader who *might* have caused trouble was executed. Some of our questions will have to remain unanswered.

About the death sentence, Marcus Borg observes that "not required by divine necessity, the execution of Jesus was virtually a human inevitability. This is what domination systems do to people who challenge them" [Borg 2006 p 273].

"GOOD FRIDAY"

The entire crucifixion story as reported in the gospels is beset by problems of historical accuracy and consistency. The various gospels do not agree on the details. There is no mention of a crucifixion in Thomas or Q. Paul reported only that Jesus was crucified. None of the disciples was around to report what happened. The flight of the disciples would have been embarrassing to the early church, so it was likely a fact that could not be dismissed. John Shelby Spong, referring to the copying from Psalm 22 and other places, notes that the lack of eyewitnesses allowed writers to create stories based on the Hebrew Testament [Spong 2007 p 113]. Details of the death scene were taken from Psalms [31:5, 69:21] and other parts of the Hebrew Testament, such as Amos 8:9 and Isaiah 53:3–12. John Dominic Crossan also discusses this [Crossan 1998 p 569]. The account in Mark of the last day is neatly—too neatly— divided into three-hour segments, a sign of creative writing.

To be sure, some of the women followers were said to witness the events, but the word of a woman in those days was not considered reliable. The women may have been added to the narratives simply to have someone witness things. But again, the gospels disagree as to who the women were.

No historical record supports the claim that a custom allowed the release of one prisoner during a festival. Even had there been such a custom, Barabbas, stated to be an insurrectionist, would certainly not have been a candidate. It is unclear why Mark, copied by Matthew and Luke, would have invented such a tale. Barabbas probably never existed. Some versions of Matthew go even further by stating that the full name of the rebel was "Jesus Barabbas." The "last name" can be broken down to "Bar Abba": "son of father," so the full name would have been "Jesus son of father." Recall that the gospels report that Yeshua sometimes referred to God as "Abba," whereby this "Jesus Barabbas" would have been "Jesus son of God," Such a tale, created after the divinity story came into being, could thus represent the wish that Jesus had been set free.

The next problem concerns when the crucifixion took place. Some scholars think the death may not have been at the time of Passover at all but during some other festival, perhaps in the fall. Even if we accept the Passover timing, the difficulty of which day remains. The problem of a trial on Passover, and the differences between John and the synoptics, are addressed above; John Meier agrees with the gospel of John and concludes that "Good Friday" was actually on a Thursday.

Carrying the cross is one of the major images of Good Friday, celebrated in paintings and in movies as part of the "Stations of the Cross." The problem with almost all of these images is that in actuality the entire cross was not carried. Only the crosspiece was; the upright was permanently in place. Some scholars say that the crosspiece was put on top of the upright, so the "cross" was more like a "T." Who carried it? The synoptic gospels say that Simon of Cyrene carried it for Jesus. This person is probably a fictional character. The gospel of John has Jesus carrying it by himself, since otherwise the call found in the gospels for "carrying your cross" would have seemed empty.

The gospels make no mention of how Jesus was fastened to the cross. The only hint comes from the later references to holes in his hands. This allusion may have been to a passage in the Hebrew Testament. Several experts contend that a person could not have been nailed through the hands because the bone structure there would not be strong enough to hold a person's weight. There is some evidence that at times the arms were tied to the crossbar, or that nails were hammered through the wrists or forearms.

Most Christians seem to think that they know the last words of Jesus. But what were they? The gospels contain four different versions, counting a second wording that appears in some of the manuscripts of Luke. Here is the list.

1. My God, my God, why did you abandon me? [Mark 15:34b and Matt 27:46b]
2. Father, into your hands I entrust my spirit. [Luke 23:46b]
3. Father, forgive them, for they don't know what they are doing. [Luke 23:34 in some versions]
4. It's all over. [John 19:30]

The first utterance was taken straight from Psalm 22:1, and the second appears in Psalm 31:5a. As already noted, quoting from the Hebrew Testament is almost a sure sign that the wording does not go back to Jesus.

According to the gospels, many extraordinary things happened at the moment of Jesus' death. In Mark, "the curtain of the Temple was torn in two" [Mark 15:38]. Matthew added three hours of darkness, as well as an earthquake that split rocks and opened tombs [Matt 27: 45, 51–52]. Luke had the darkness and a curtain tearing. John had no special signs. These events must be viewed as creative writing, as there is no independent mention of such things happening. Paul makes no mention of any of these special signs: the death happened without fanfare.

IMMEDIATELY AFTER

What happened after Jesus' death? In a Roman crucifixion, the body was usually left on the cross to rot or become carrion, or it was thrown into a lime pit to decompose. The Romans' final twist of the knife was the denial of a burial, since immediate burial before sundown was an important part of the Jewish tradition. We saw in chapter 2 that one entombed crucified body has been found, which indicates that a burial was not out of the question, though the interpretation of these remains is controversial. Apparently this victim was either nailed through his arms or tied to the cross.

But was there a tomb? Jesus' burial by Joseph of Arimathea is likely a fabrication by Mark. It is possible that Jesus was placed in a nearby tomb as the gospels state, to honor the Jewish burial tradition. If so, this would have been a temporary expedient, since according to the gospels night was falling. In this case the body might soon have been moved to another location, whence the empty tomb story might have arisen. The foregoing is all quite speculative. Many scholars think that there was no burial and the empty tomb story was a creation of Mark to validate the resurrection myth.

Death by crucifixion was often slow, but Jesus is said to have died rather quickly. It has been speculated that he was not really dead when he was removed from the cross and ultimately survived. If there were any truth to this theory, it would explain much of the subsequent "appearances" mythology.

The Christian Testament talks of "rising after three days," although the interval was only from Friday afternoon to Sunday morning, according to the synoptics. The phrase "on the third day" was used in some places to get around this problem. The "three days" figure probably goes back to the custom of not being declared dead until after three days, as discussed in chapter 8. Anything sooner would have left the gospels open to the criticism "Well, he wasn't really dead because three days had not passed." The phrase "on the third day" and even the resurrection may come from Hosea 6:2: "After two days he will revive us; on the third day he will raise us up, that we may live before him." Another problem with the "third day" is the passage in Luke where one of the criminals allegedly crucified with Jesus asks for mercy: "And he implored, 'Jesus, remember me when you come into your domain.' And Jesus said to him, 'I swear to you, *today* you'll be with me in paradise.'" [Luke 23:42–43, emphasis added] This passage would imply going to heaven immediately that day, not after three days.

INTERPRETING "DYING FOR OUR SINS"

"Christ died for our sins" [1 Cor 15:3b, for example] is one of the most common Christian statements. Borg and Crossan go into great detail to explain that this statement has been distorted from Paul's original meaning [Borg and Crossan ch 5]. According to Borg and Crossan the real significance of the crucifixion and resurrection, for Paul, was the end of the Roman "peace through victory" ushering in a change to a "peace through justice" (see their book for the full discussion). Marcus Borg notes, "The notion that God's only son came to this planet to offer his life as a sacrifice for the sins of the world, and that God could not forgive us without that having happened, and that we are saved by believing this story, *is simply incredible*" [Borg 1994 p 131, emphasis added].

The concept of "dying for our sins" totally turns Yeshua's ideas of God upside down. Paul was likely responsible for this. According to James Robinson, "in Paul's thinking, the God of infinite love, still echoed in the traditions going back to Jesus, was combined with the scriptural traditions of the just God obliged to avenge evil. The result was the concept of a *loving God* sending his Son to placate a *God wrathful* over sin" [Robinson p 215, emphasis added]. Marcus Borg, commenting on the concept of dying for sins, says, "It limits God by saying God can forgive sins only if adequate payment is made" [Borg 2006 p 270]. The Torah prohibits the sacrifice of a child, which leads Wayne-Daniel Berard to conclude that the idea of God sacrificing his own son as an offering to himself would not be acceptable to a Jew [Berard pp 221–222].

Paul elaborated on the sacrificial idea: "For our paschal lamb, Christ, has been sacrificed" [1 Cor 5:7b]. Here, with the word "paschal," Paul did reference Passover. A lamb was the standard sacrificial animal for that festival, so Jesus became the "Lamb of God." This expression may have been created to soften the image of God requiring a human sacrifice.

Some of a passage in Isaiah (53:5–12) could also be a source of "dying for our sins":

> **But he was wounded for our transgressions, crushed for our iniquities; upon him was the punishment that made us whole, and by his bruises we are healed...The righteous one, my servant, shall make many righteous, and he shall bear their iniquities...Yet he bore the sin of many.**[6]

John Dominic Crossan is, in my judgment, the best source of details about "dying for our sins" [Crossan 1998 pp 440–441, 503 and Crossan 1991 pp 386–387]. The idea appears also to have a basis in the idea of the scapegoat, the goat driven out of the city and killed to atone for sins [Lev 16:7–10]. Passages in 4 Maccabees (likely written between the years 19 and 54 CE and thus before the earliest gospel) depict martyrs purifying the land by freeing it from foreign control, thus becoming "a ransom for the sin of our nation":

....
6 Some interpreters say that this passage refers to the Jewish nation as a whole and not an individual.

They vindicated their nation. [4 Macc 17:10a]
They have become, as it were, a ransom for the sin of our nation. And through the blood of those devout ones and their death as an atoning sacrifice, divine Providence preserved Israel that previously had been mistreated. [4 Macc 17:21b–22]

RESURRECTION

It is important to understand what was meant by the word "resurrection," since it is often considered the same as raising the dead. Resurrection in this context was *not* a coming back to an ordinary mortal life merely to face death again, but rather a transformation into some new existence. However, there are some conflicting statements by Paul (see below). The empty tomb story does seem to imply that the body was raised.

Death on a cross was not supposed to happen to a leader who preached peace. Instead of the movement dying with its leader, as so often happened, some of Yeshua's followers gathered to keep his message alive. In doing so, they enabled their leader to "live on" in their hearts. For me, this is one meaning of Easter: a person remembered after death. It goes along with the Buddhist concept of "no birth, no death."

Most Unitarian Universalists, I believe, view Easter as the rebirth of nature in springtime and a celebration of life in general. Easter is closely tied to pagan ideas. First, the name comes from the pagan spring (or dawn) goddess Eastre. The early church found it expedient to tie into pagan rites by co-opting the springtime festival held in her honor. Our modern celebration of Easter makes many references to the pagan rites of spring. The Western Christian churches' timing of Easter is based on just the spring equinox and the full moon, very pagan.[7] The egg and the rabbit are symbols of fertility. Newly blossoming flowers show the return of life. The Easter lily is a symbol of life as well as death.

The resurrection is *the* crucial point for Christianity. It is *the* central belief. It really comes down to faith versus rationality. You believe or you don't.

----

7 The Eastern Orthodox Church adds the requirement that Easter must be *after* Passover.

The origins of the resurrection myth remain murky. Paul played a big role in promulgating this myth, and it is possible he even invented it. Chapter 2 covers some of the creativity of Paul. Several theories attempt to explain the start of the resurrection myth. John Dominic Crossan states, "If those who accepted Jesus during his earthly life had not continued to follow, believe, and experience his continuing presence after the crucifixion, all would have been over. *That* is the resurrection" [Crossan 1991 p 404, emphasis added]. James Robinson states that it was the Easter myth that *created* the various stories such as the empty tomb and the post-death appearances, not the other way around [Robinson p 207]. So it would appear that the start of the resurrection myth might have been with Yeshua's followers still believing in his central message. In this sense, he lived on.

I have this problem with the resurrection: if it did happen, why would God have hidden it? If he wanted people to believe, wouldn't he have done it publicly, with a big flash of light or something, during the day while everyone was watching? Either God needed better PR, or he truly worked in totally mysterious ways, or it was all fiction.

In many places the gospels quote Jesus predicting his death and resurrection. If he had actually said he would be resurrected as many times he is stated to have done in the synoptics, it is impossible to imagine that his followers would have fled. Instead, we would have expected them to wait around to celebrate this wondrous event. To be sure, they would have been fearful of being caught by the Romans and crucified. But this was not enough of an excuse for missing *the* event of all time. Even the reports of the behavior of the women on finding an empty tomb are not compatible with their knowing a prediction about "rising from the dead." So we must consider all of those resurrection predictions to be creations of Mark and the later writers.

References to a general life after death in the Hebrew Testament are almost entirely confined to books written after about 200 BCE, although in earlier books some people are said to have been taken directly up to heaven—Elijah and Enoch, for example. The concept of a bodily resurrection had been formulated by the second century BCE but was not generally accepted. The Pharisees in the first century CE believed in an afterlife, but that was not a common notion in Judaism at that time. The Sadducees did not believe in resurrections.

There are conflicting ideas about whether or not resurrection applied to the physical body. Paul said in some places that only a spiritual body was raised, not the physical. For example, there is this passage:

What is sown is perishable, what is raised is imperishable... It is sown a physical body, it is raised a spiritual body. [1 Cor 15:42b, 44]

In other places, Paul seems to have had a different view. For example, he also stated [Rom 8:11b] "...[God] will give life to your mortal bodies..."

Resurrection ideas were common in Greco-Roman mythologies. No bones were found when Hercules, the son of Zeus, died. The list of people going to heaven is long: Apollo's son Aristaeus, Aeneas, Romulus, Empedocles, and Apollonius, just to mention a few. Robert Price covers the issue in more detail [Price pp 286–289 and pp 334–336].

More contemporary to the time of Jesus was the Romans' belief that their emperors rose to heaven. Caesar was said in 42 BCE to be divine and to have risen to heaven. Later, Julius Caesar's adopted son Augustus was also declared divine after his death in 14 CE. So for the Romans there was nothing special about a leader rising from the dead and becoming divine.

Paul gives a rather weak argument to support the resurrection.

Now if Christ is proclaimed as raised from the dead, how can some of you say there is no resurrection of the dead? If there is no resurrection of the dead, then Christ has not been raised; and if Christ has not been raised, then our proclamation has been in vain and your faith has been in vain...But in fact Christ has been raised from the dead, the first fruits of those who have died. [1 Cor 15:12–20]

In one view, understanding the origin of the resurrection myth starts with the martyr tradition. As the various "Jesus groups" were trying to spread the word, they found they needed to legitimize themselves. A commonly executed troublemaker would not do as the source of their message. So they turned to the Greek idea of the "noble death." Being a martyr to a cause, holding steadfastly to it in the face of death, validated the person and the cause. Socrates was a very notable example. Other examples of noble martyrs are found in 2 Maccabees 7, the story of seven brothers and their mother who all suffered torture and chose death rather than betray their faith.

Martyrs usually die for an established cause. In this case, the cause was new, so something more was needed for the story. I speculate that the resurrection myth originated out of practical necessity. Yeshua often talked about the coming "Kingdom of God," but he died the death reserved for treason before anything happened. How could he have left things undone? Harking back possibly to Elijah, his followers may have expected Yeshua to come back to finish the work. But how could he come back unless he had been raised bodily to heaven?

Burton Mack, in *Who Wrote the New Testament? The Making of the Christian Myth*, takes a different approach to extending the martyrdom. He says that being a martyr was not enough for a new cause: the martyr himself had to be vindicated [Mack 1995 p 84]. So the story was created that since Jesus was faithful to God, God exalted his death as a sign of that faithfulness by raising him from the dead. Geza Vermes agrees that the resurrection was needed to vindicate the death of Jesus [Vermes 2000 p 96]—or at least the *story* of the resurrection was needed.

Some other possible sources of the resurrection myth include a Jewish wisdom tale about the vindication of a falsely charged righteous man [Wis 2:12–20] and the Greek concepts of hero and divine man [Mack 1995 pp 78–87, 92–94; see also Mack 1993 p 217–219]. Paul may have relied heavily on the Greek idea of a dead and risen hero who had been part human and part god. In addition, several scholars have noted that the idea of a "suffering messiah" existed in some Jewish circles in the years before the birth of Yeshua. See my chapter 2 and *The Messiah Before Jesus* by Israel Knohl. Pointedly, the stone tablet of "Gabriel's Revelation" (mentioned in chapter 2) features the "in three days you shall live" language. Jesus' suffering on the cross invites comparison with the earlier tradition of a "suffering messiah."

Other writers think that the "sightings" of Jesus after he died possibly led to the resurrection myth. These visions were and are firmly believed by the Christian church. But the Christian Testament's account of the post-resurrection appearances is marred by major disagreement over when and to whom. Paul had a long list; see the endnote in chapter 3. Mark recorded no appearances in his gospel (in the un-appended version), but he did include a statement that the disciples should go to Galilee for one. Matthew had a single visionary appearance in Galilee. According to Luke, the disciples stayed in Jerusalem, and the appearances were there and also on the road to Emmaus. John wrote of appearances in Jerusalem and perhaps in Galilee (the latter is in John 21, which was likely added by a later writer).

Did people really see these visions? We do not know. However, psychology recognizes that people often think they see or feel the presence of a recently departed person. Stacy Davids states that about 50 to 80 percent of bereaved people feel the "presence" or "spirit" of a person who has died [Crossan 1998 p xvi].

HOW JESUS GOT HIS "LAST NAME"

The origin of the designation "Christ" is not clear to me.[8] Not even the resurrection of a dead person was enough to start a new religion. Even Luke noted this: "If they do not listen to Moses and the prophets, neither will they be convinced even if someone rises from the dead"[9] [Luke 16:31]. So the followers had to invent a better story. To compete with Roman theology, Jesus had to be at least a "Son of God." I believe that the usage of "Christ" got started with the use of "Son of God," with capitals as a title. Note that some of the earliest manuscripts did not use "Son of God," but rather "Chosen One."

It is fascinating to see how the designation of "sonhood" develops in the Christian Testament as the writings unfold chronologically. Paul was the first to record it. It is possible that Paul invented the whole "divine, son of God, God, and Lord" designations specifically in order to compete with the Emperor Augustus, on whom the same designations were conferred. In Paul's letters, we find that becoming God's son happened at the time of Jesus' resurrection: "...and was declared to be Son of God with power according to the spirit of holiness *by resurrection from the dead*" [Rom 1:4, emphasis added]. Similar statements are found in Acts 2:36 and 13:33. However, Paul presented an inconsistent view, since he also stated that Jesus was a man and the preexistent Son of God who came down, ascended, and will come again.

The next chronological step, moving the attainment of "sonhood" to an earlier time in Jesus' life, is found in Mark, where it happened right

---

8 I am making a distinction between "Christ" with its divine associations and "christ," the translation of "anointed person."

9 However, this passage was in another context, where the reference was to Lazarus.

after his baptism by John the Baptizer. "There was a voice from the skies: 'You are my favored son—I fully approve of you'" [Mark 1:11]. In this case, no one else heard the voice.

The origin of this sonhood is likely the Psalms, where it is stated that every king became a son of God upon his anointment: "You are my son; today I have begotten you" [Ps 2:7b]. Another possible influence on the "son of God" designation is that in the Hebrew Testament, all Israelites are called the children of God, though without any divine connotations [Vermes 2000 p 3].

Matthew and Luke, in their birth stories, placed the "sonhood" at the moment of conception.

Finally, John said that Jesus was always related to God.

> In the beginning there was the divine word and wisdom...The divine word and wisdom became human and made itself home among us. We have seen its majesty, majesty appropriate to a Father's only son. [John 1:1, 14]

I speculate that the first step to "Christ" was the "sonhood." Next, this has to link with "messiah." As already noted, originally this term meant "anointed," as in the case of kings, and did not imply divinity. But for some people under Roman occupation, the term "messiah" became associated with someone who would lead the Israelites to victory over the Romans. This person would be a warrior-king like David and thus a savior in that sense. Jesus' followers could reasonably have thought that a political overthrow of the Roman rulers was part of the coming "Kingdom of God" and may thus have considered Jesus a potential messiah.

Translated into Greek, messiah became "christos." Barrie Wilson suggests that something was altered in that transition, especially as used by Paul. In Hebrew "messiah" referred to a fully human anointed person. Paul gave the word "christos" overtones of a Greco-Roman dying-rising hero [Wilson pp 178–179], and the designation "christos" became a title: "Christos." Strictly, the usage of "Christ" should read "Jesus the Christ." This is often shortened to a "last name" as in "Jesus Christ."

Burton Mack states that the justification for the "Christ" label was Jesus' obeying "God's will" by accepting death [Mack 1995 p 92]. Paula Fredriksen has a similar idea: "With the claim made soon after his death that Jesus was the messiah, his death had to be explained. Crucifixion confirmed Jesus' status within Christian tradition only in light of the faith in his resurrection. It is this faith that moved the early proclama-tion from 'Jesus is messiah *despite* his death on the cross' to 'Jesus is messiah *because of* his death on the cross'" [Fredriksen p 110, emphasis in original].

SECOND COMING

The "second coming" may have been Paul's brainchild. In the sec-tion on Resurrection above, I suggested that the belief that the prophet Elijah would someday come again could have been the inspiration for this expectation in the case of Jesus. About a "second coming," E. P. Sanders raises the interesting point that it is uncertain whether Jesus was speaking of himself when he spoke of a future "son of Adam com-ing on a cloud." He might have been referring to yet another prophet or messiah to come [Sanders pp 247–248; see also Weyler p 217]. Others think that "son of Adam" referred to the entire Jewish state, implying freedom from Rome. Of course, it is highly unlikely that Yeshua ever referred to a "son of Adam coming on a cloud." The Jesus Seminar held this passage to be inauthentic. As a quote from the Book of Daniel, it is immediately suspected to be an insertion by the gospel writers.

TRINITY

No Jew would have entertained the idea that a person could be equal to god. Jesus certainly would never have thought so. God is singular.

Several references in the book called John show that Jesus, as the son, was a lesser figure than God [5:19–20, 7:16, and 14:28]. The clear-est example is, "Because the Father is greater than I am" [14:28b] The Didache seems to say that Jesus was less than God by using the expres-sion "your servant Jesus" [Milavec pp 23–25].

The idea that Jesus was a lesser figure was also true for Paul. Geza Vermes notes that Paul regularly addressed prayers to God and not di-rectly to Jesus (but sometimes through Jesus). Jesus, even as the son of god, was not god in Paul's mind. Vermes cites many passages in Paul in support of this statement [Vermes 2000 p 87–88]. Vermes adds that there is nothing in the Acts of the Apostles that implies a divine Jesus [Vermes 2000 p 156]. Karen Armstrong agrees, saying that Paul was too Jewish to accept the idea of Christ as another divinity alongside God

[Armstrong 1993 p 88]. Mark never thought of Jesus as an incarnation of God but only as the adopted son. In Mark [10:18], "'Why do you call me good? No one is good except for God alone,'" we see a lesser role. See also the discussion of Robert Price [p 118–119].

The concept of the trinity, "God the Father, the Son and the Holy Ghost," is central to Christianity. It can come as a surprise that this concept is not in the bible, although in places the three names are invoked, for example in Matthew: "You are to baptize them in the name of the Father and the son and the holy spirit" [Matt 28:19b]. This passage in Matthew seems to imply a triple baptism, invoking three separate names. Another possibility is that this sentence was added to Matthew after the doctrine of the trinity was adopted. The Council of Nicaea formally deified Jesus to full godhood in 325 CE. The concept of the trinity evolved only slowly, and its varied interpretation was partially responsible for the split between the Eastern and Western Catholic churches. The exact meaning of the trinity is still debated. Tracing the full development of the trinity concept would take us too far afield; see Karen Armstrong for a more thorough discussion [1993 ch 4].

THE SPREAD OF CHRISTIANITY

I had often wondered how Christianity spread so quickly and widely throughout the Roman Empire. Did this spread imply something special that I was missing? This question was one of several that got me started on this long journey. However, I now see that Christianity's rise is comparable to the rise of Buddhism, Islam, Taoism, and Confucianism, which all originated with a single free-thinking person and spread widely within 200 years or so. The recent rise of Mormonism is another example. In this perspective, the rise of Christianity need not be viewed as an indication of some special status for Jesus. Yeshua, of course, never called for a new religion and especially not anything in his name.

The first followers saw Yeshua as an example to emulate. The next generation saw Jesus as a god figure that they could not imitate. So the emerging church changed its emphasis to the messenger and not his message.

The biggest factor in the spread of what became Christianity was Paul's major repackaging and selling of it to the gentiles. He cleverly eliminated all requirements for keeping the Law, and he added elements of the Greco-Roman mystery religions, which were familiar to the gentiles already. But he kept a tie all the way back to Abraham of the Hebrew Testament to make it seem that his was an ancient religion and not something new.

Barrie Wilson's book *How Jesus Became Christian* details this transformation. The Pauline church started its early spread in the synagogues of the diaspora, especially those with gentile associates. Paul's statement that gentiles need not convert to Judaism brought about a split from the Jews, whereupon recruitment of the gentiles became more successful. Many gentiles found elements of Judaism appealing. Its single God of justice was a welcome relief from the many capricious gods and goddesses of the Greek and Roman traditions. What had stopped many from converting was the strict Law. Circumcision as an adult was an especial barrier, with the food laws following closely behind. The more relaxed requirements of Paul's Christianity allowed gentiles to participate with ease.

The newly emerging church had many appealing aspects. Because of its initial acceptance of women, many of the early converts to Christianity were women who were then able to persuade the rest of the family to convert as well. Conversion to Christianity was often found along family lines and in social networks. The lowest class of people found support in the community. The belief of a better life yet to come was an attractive concept, especially when they were promised that it would happen soon. People found a caring and sharing community in the early church. Probably the idea of caring for others in the community led to better health care and a decreased mortality rate, increasing the congregants' numbers.

Rodney Stark believes that the expansion of Christianity hinged on attracting people of a higher echelon—the more educated people. If recruitment had been limited to the lowest classes, the new church would have been squashed as a political movement [Stark 1996 p 46]. It was also very important that people who could read and write join the movement.

A little compound growth arithmetic shows that only modest annual growth would result in a significant number. Let's assume that there were about 500 Jesus followers in the year 40 CE. If the growth rate was only 3 percent per year, then by the year 300 there would have been over one million members of what by then was called Christianity. For a much more thorough treatment, see *The Rise of Christianity* by Rodney Stark.

Appendix

IDEAS FOR USE IN ADULT RELIGIOUS EDUCATION

Many people raised as Unitarian Universalists know little about Yeshua, the person. If they came from a trinitarian church, they often know a lot about "Christ" but little about the human teacher. Of course, previously unchurched people have almost no knowledge of Yeshua. This book can be the basis for an Adult Religious Education program to help inform these people about Yeshua.

I used an earlier version of this book as the text for a six-week Adult Religious Education Class at the Unitarian Universalist Congregation in Milford (NH). The classes covered the material as follows:

1. An introduction, where people talked about what they expected to get out of this course. We watched the first hour of the PBS show, *From Jesus to Christ* and discussed its contents. The text was distributed.
2. Chapters 1 and 2.
3. Chapter 3.
4. Chapter 4. The course could profitably spend two weeks on this chapter by adding an extra week or reducing the time spent elsewhere.
5. Chapters 5 and 6.
6. "But What About…?" (chapters 7, 8 and 9).

A one-session class could focus on just chapter 6 and the meaning of Jesus for today. A two-week class might discuss just chapter 4. A four-week class could focus on chapters 3 through 6. A five-week class could be based on chapters 3–6 and 8. You get the idea.

There are other ways to structure a course on Yeshua. Two to six weeks could be profitably spent by selecting just a few of the sayings from chapters 4 and 5 and discussing each in depth. What follows is a sample of suggested sayings. Some are worth a full class, while others could be combined in a single session. The ordering of the list has no significance. Please feel free to make your own selections.

1. Golden Rule [Luke 6:31]
2. Good Samaritan [Luke 10:30–35]
3. Prodigal Son [Luke 15:11–32]
4. Vineyard Workers [Matt 20:1–16]
5. Leaven [Matt 13:33]
6. Mustard Seed [Thom 20:2–3 ‖ Luke 17:20–21]
7. Empty Jar [Thom 97:1–4]
8. Love Enemies [Matt 5:44–46]
9. Turn Cheek, Walk Mile, Give Cloak [Matt 5:39–41]
10. Lost Sheep [Matt 18:12–13] and Lost Coin [Luke 15:8–9]
11. Wine Skins, Patches [Luke 5:36–39]
12. Wash the Cup on the Outside [Thom 89:1–2 ‖ Matt 23:25–26]
13. Dead Bury the Dead [Matt 8:22]
14. Hidden Treasure, Priceless Pearl [Matt 13:44–46]
15. Snakes and Doves [Thom 39:3 ‖ Matt 10:16]

Recommended resources for the parables and sayings are:
  Listening to the Parables of Jesus, Edward Beutner, ed.
  Re-Imagine the World, Bernard Brandon Scott
  The Five Gospels, The Jesus Seminar

In the following list, I provide some suggestions for discussion of some of the above sayings.

Golden Rule [Luke 6:31 ‖ Matt 7:12]
Altogether, there are four ways to state the Golden Rule (see chapter 4). Discuss the four versions and the pros and cons of each, creating your own listing.
- What are your thoughts?
- What about self-defense?
- Discuss and formulate an alternative Golden Rule that works for you (or for UUs in general).

The Good Samaritan [Luke 10:30–35]
- What is the likelihood of this being authentic?
- Does this condemn the Jewish leaders?
- What might it have meant in Galilee at that time?
- Does it go beyond being a good neighbor (which was the context in Luke)?

Prodigal Son [Luke 15:11–32]
- What do you think when you hear a person being called "prodigal"?
- What is the surface meaning? What could be a deeper meaning?
- Put yourself in the shoes of the older son.

Vineyard Workers [Matt 20:1–16]
- What can we possibly make of the uneven work/rewards? Where is fairness?
- Is it a comment on the difficult economy of the times?

Leaven [Matt 13:33]
- Leaven was considered unclean. How does this affect your understanding?

Mustard Seed [Thom 20:2–3 || Matt 13:31–32]
- A mustard plant grows like a weed. So what can we understand?

Empty Jar [Thom 97:1–4]
- How does an empty jar relate to the kingdom of god?

Another interesting class would be to collect as many versions of the Lord's Prayer as you can find (look up one or more translated Aramaic versions) and discuss the differences and meanings, then try to formulate a version that fits your Unitarian Universalist beliefs.

These are of course just suggestions and ideas to help you formulate your own class.

Bibliography

Akers, Keith. *The Lost Religion of Jesus*. Lantern Books, New York, 2000

Armstrong, Karen. *A History of God*. Random House Publishing, New York, 1993

———. *Buddha*. Penguin Putnam, New York, 2001

———. *The Bible: A Biography*. Atlantic Monthly Press, New York, 2007

Berard, Wayne-Daniel. *When Christians Were Jews (That Is, Now)*. Cowley Publications, Cambridge, MA, 2006

Beutner, Edward F., editor. *Listening to the Parables of Jesus*. Polebridge Press, Santa Rosa, CA, 2007

Borg, Marcus J. *Meeting Jesus Again for the First Time*. HarperSanFrancisco, San Francisco, 1994

———. *Jesus*. HarperSanFrancisco, San Francisco, 2006

Borg, Marcus J. and John Dominic Crossan. *The First Paul*. HarperOne, New York, 2009

Bumbaugh, David E. *Unitarian Universalism, a Narrative History*. Meadville Lombard Theological School Press, Chicago, 2000

Chilton, Bruce. *Rabbi Jesus*. Doubleday, New York, 2000

Carus, Paul. *The Gospel of Buddha*. Senate, an imprint of Random House, London, 1995

Crossan, John Dominic. *The Historical Jesus*. HarperSanFrancisco, San Francisco, 1991

———. *Jesus: A Revolutionary Biography*. HarperSanFrancisco, San Francisco, 1994

———. *The Birth of Christianity*. HarperSanFrancisco, San Francisco, 1998

Crossan, John Dominic and Jonathan L. Reed. *Excavating Jesus*. HarperSanFrancisco, San Francisco, 2001

Ehrman, Bart D. *Lost Scriptures*. Oxford University Press, New York, 2003

———. *Misquoting Jesus*. HarperSanFrancisco, San Francisco, CA, 2005

Fredriksen, Paula. *From Jesus to Christ* (second edition). Yale University Press, New Haven , CT, 2000

Funk, Robert W. *Honest to Jesus*. HarperSanFrancisco, San Francisco, 1996

——— (with The Jesus Seminar). *The Acts of Jesus*. HarperSanFrancisco, San Francisco, 1998

Funk, Robert W. and Roy W. Hoover (with The Jesus Seminar). *The Five Gospels*. HarperSanFrancisco, San Francisco, 1993

Gomes, Peter J. *The Scandalous Gospel of Jesus*. HarperCollins Publishers, New York, 2007

Gulley, Philip. *If the Church Were Christian*. HarperOne, New York, 2010

Hanh, Thich Nhat. *Touching Peace*. Parallax Press, Berkeley, CA, 1992

Helms, Randel McCraw. *Who Wrote the Gospels?* Millennium Press, Altadena, CA, 1997

Hendricks Jr., Obery M. *The Politics of Jesus*. Doubleday, New York, 2006

Jacobovici, Simcha and Charles Pellegrino. *The Jesus Family Tomb*. HarperSanFrancisco, San Francisco, 2007

Jesus Seminar. *The Once and Future Jesus*. Polebridge Press, Santa Rosa, CA, 2000

Levine, Amy-Jill, Dale C. Allison Jr., and John Dominic Crossan, editors. *The Historical Jesus in Context*. Princeton University Press, Princeton, NJ, 2006

Mack, Burton L. *The Lost Gospel of Q*. HarperSanFrancisco, San Francisco, 1993

———. *Who Wrote the New Testament?* Harper Collins, New York, 1995

McLennan, Scotty. *Jesus Was A Liberal*. Palgrave Macmillan, New York, 2009

Meier, John P. *A Marginal Jew* (three volumes). Doubleday, New York, 1991, 1994, 2001

Meyers, Robin. *Why the Religious Right is Wrong*. John Wiley & Sons, San Francisco, 2006

———. *Saving Jesus from the Church*. HarperOne. New York, 2009

Milavec, Aaron. *The Didache*. Liturgical Press, Collegeville, MN, 2003

Moyers, Bill. *Healing and The Mind*. Doubleday, New York, 1993

Miller, Robert J., editor. *The Complete Gospels*. Polebridge Press, Salem, OR, 1992

Price, Robert M. *The Incredible Shrinking Son of Man.* Prometheus Books, Amherst, NY, 2003

Rasor, Paul. *Faith Without Certainty.* Skinner House Books, Boston, MA, 2005

Robinson, James M. *The Gospel of Jesus.* HarperSanFrancisco, San Francisco, 2005

Rolenz, Kathleen, editor: *Christian Voices in Unitarian Universalism.* Skinner House Books, Boston, MA, 2006

Sanders, E. P. *The Historical Figure of Jesus.* Penguin Books, London, 1995

Shanks, Hershel, editor. *Where Christianity Was Born.* Biblical Archaeology Society, Washington DC, 2006

———. *Ancient Israel, Third Edition.* Biblical Archaeology Society, Washington DC, 2011

Siegel, Bernie. *Peace, Love, and Healing.* HarperPerennial, New York, 1993

Smith, Huston. *The World's Religions.* HarperSanFrancisco, San Francisco, 1991

Spong, John Shelby. *Liberating the Gospels.* HarperSanFrancisco, San Francisco, 1996

———. *Jesus for the Non-religious.* HarperSanFrancisco, San Francisco, 2007

Stark, Rodney. *The Rise of Christianity.* HarperSanFrancisco, San Francisco, 1996

———. *Discovering God.* HarperOne, New York, 2007

Tabor, James D. *The Jesus Dynasty.* Simon & Schuster, New York, 2006

Vermes, Geza. *The Changing Faces of Jesus.* Penguin Books, London, 2000

———. *Jesus in His Jewish Context.* Fortress Press, Minneapolis, MN, 2003

———. *The Authentic Gospel of Jesus.* Penguin Books, London, 2004

Wakefield, Dan. *The Hijacking of Jesus.* Avalon Publishing Group, New York, 2006

Wallis, Jim. *God's Politics.* HarperCollins, New York, 2005

Weyler, Rex. *The Jesus Sayings.* House of Anansi Press, Toronto, 2008

White, L. Michael. *From Jesus to Christianity.* HarperSanFrancisco, San Francisco, 2004

Wilkinson, Richard and Kate Pickett. *The Spirit Level.* Bloomsbury Press, New York, 2010

Wikstrom, Erik Walker. *Teacher, Guide, Companion: Rediscovering Jesus in a Secular World.* Skinner House Books, Boston, MA, 2004

Wilson, Barrie. *How Jesus Became Christian.* St. Martin's Press, New York, 2008

www.ingramcontent.com/pod-product-compliance
Lightning Source LLC
Chambersburg PA
CBHW052046090426
42739CB00010B/2065